Towards a new social compact for care in old age

Edited by Janice Robinson

Published by
King's Fund Publishing
11–13 Cavendish Square
London W1G 0AN

© King's Fund 2001

First published 2001

ISBN 1 85717 444 5

A CIP catalogue record for this book is available from the British Library

Available from:
King's Fund Bookshop
11–13 Cavendish Square
London
W1G 0AN
Tel: 020 7307 2591
Fax: 020 7307 2801

Printed and bound in Great Britain

Cover illustration: Minuche Mazumdar Farrar

Towar

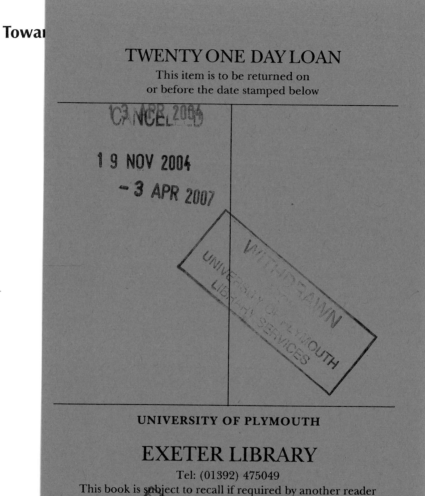

Contents

Contributors

CHRIS DEEMING is a Research Officer at the King's Fund. Prior to taking up this post he worked within the NHS as an information and policy analyst as well as leading a variety of health service development projects. Since joining the King's Fund just over a year ago, he has led two studies on long-term care funding: *Paying for old age?* (King's Fund, 2000), *A fair deal for older people? Public views on the funding of long-term care* (King's Fund, 2001). He has also written on the politics of long-term care funding (*Health Care UK: Spring 2001*, King's Fund, 2001).

JUSTIN KEEN is Professor of Health Politics and Information Management at the Nuffield Institute for Health, University of Leeds. Prior to taking up this post, he was a Fellow in Health Systems at the King's Fund, where he worked on a range of topics related to the funding of public services, including the funding of long-term care. During 1996–8, he worked at the National Audit Office, having been seconded from Brunel University, where he had worked for ten years in the Health Economics Research Group and then in the Department of Government.

HILARY LAND has been Professor of Family Policy and Child Welfare at the University of Bristol since 1995. Before that she was Professor of Social Policy at Royal Holloway College, University of London. Her long-standing interest in family policies started in the 1960s, when working with Professors Abel-Smith and Townsend at the London School of Economics on a national study of poverty. Hilary Land has written extensively on State policies concerning and supporting relationships and responsibilities within the family, between young and old as well as between men and women. This has been done using both comparative and historical perspectives and has been informed by the debates instigated by the second-wave feminists in the 1970s. She has always been interested in the application of research in the policy-making process, and during 1979–80 was an adviser to the Central Policy Review Staff in the Cabinet Office. Recent publications include (with Jane Lewis and Kathleen Kiernan) *Lone motherhood in twentieth-century Britain* (Oxford University Press, 1999). Professor Land is currently working on a study of contemporary family policies in Britain.

ROBIN MEANS is Associate Dean (Primary and Community Care) at the Faculty of Health and Social Care, University of the West of England, Bristol. He has written extensively on community care issues and is co-author of both *Community care: policy and practice* (Macmillan, 1998) and *From Poor Law to community care* (Policy Press, 1998). He was lead author of *Making partnerships work in community care: a guide for practitioners in housing, health and social services* (Policy Press, 1997), which became official practice guidance for both the Department of Health and the DETR. He also contributed to Research Volume Two of the Royal Commission on Long Term Care in terms of the importance of housing and housing organisations to meeting long-term care needs. His present research includes work on rehabilitation, the history of community care services from 1971 to 1993, and dementia care issues.

RAYMOND PLANT was appointed Professor of European Political Thought at the University of Southampton in 2000. Prior to this, from 1994–2000, he was Master of St Catherine's College, Oxford. He has been a Labour member of the House of Lords since 1992. His publications include: *Community and ideology* (Routledge, 1974), *Hegel* (2nd ed., Blackwell, 1983), *Citizenship, rights and socialism* (Fabian Society, 1988), *Conservative capitalism in Britain and the USA* (with K Hoover, Routledge, 1988), *Modern political thought* (Blackwell, 1991), and *Politics, theology and history* (Cambridge University Press, 2001).

JANICE ROBINSON is Director of the Health and Social Care Programme at the King's Fund. She has a background in social policy and has a special interest in disability and ageing, and in developments promoting independent living. She has worked in statutory and voluntary organisations, undertaking research, and leading a variety of community care service and policy development initiatives. At the King's Fund she leads a team working to improve the integration of care and support for people with continuing health and social care needs. Current projects focus on provision for vulnerable older people and their carers, and for younger adults with mental health problems; on partnerships between health and social services; and on the care workforce.

Chapter 1

Long-term care in the twenty-first century

Janice Robinson

In the latter part of the twentieth century, public and political dissatisfaction with the funding and provision of care services increased dramatically. Three major inquiries were undertaken: by the Joseph Rowntree Foundation,[1] the House of Commons Health Select Committee,[2] and the Royal Commission on Long Term Care.[3] There was a remarkable degree of consensus within these inquiries that the current system of long-term care was complicated and confusing to users, unfair on people with chronic illness and disability, and characterised by unacceptable variations in quality, access and availability of services across the country.[4] By the time the Royal Commission issued its report, expectations were high that a fundamental reform might be imminent. The system of long-term care that arose in the 1940s was now seen to be outdated and unfit for the twenty-first century.

The Labour government, which had established the Royal Commission, accepted many of the Commission's recommendations, particularly those concerned with raising the standards of care in both residential and domiciliary services. However, recommendations concerned with funding long-term care were largely resisted or deferred for further consultations. Thus, while the Government agreed to make nursing care free in nursing homes (as it is in hospitals and community services), it decided to maintain means-testing for personal care and all other aspects of long-term care. It agreed to look into ways of reducing variations in local authority charges for care services and of improving protection through insurance and savings products for those people who 'may still worry about possible care costs'.[5] The Government set out its position on long-term care in its NHS Plan,[6] locating its proposals for change within a wider vision of modernising health and social care services to be 'fit for the 21st century'. As far as its proposals for long-term care were concerned, these fell far short of the reforms needed.

Labour's modern system of long-term care will, in many vital respects, look like the system that emerged after the Second World War. Important changes have been made: with the introduction of legislation to end the anomaly about charges for nursing care in nursing homes; the establishment of new institutions whose role is to raise the quality of care through regulation and support the implementation of National Service Frameworks; and with the development of more rehabilitative services that should prevent unnecessary use of long-term care. However, the system of funding long-term care remains essentially unchanged from that which emerged in the post-war settlement. This system is built on a distinction between health care (which is free and financed through general taxation) and social care (which is means-tested). The question has to be asked whether this amounts to a system that fits the economic, social and political conditions of a society that is very different to the one that existed half a century ago. There are also questions as to whether the changes introduced by Labour are understood and accepted by the public at large, whether they are sustainable in the short to medium term, and whether we can expect new calls for further reforms in the near future. This short collection of papers considers these questions.

What is undeniably true is that there is a good deal of unease about the funding of long-term care among the major political parties. It remains to be seen whether differences of view within and between these parties will become more apparent during 2001 – the year of a general election. The Liberal Democrat Party has voiced its support for making personal care free to all who need it.[7] The Conservative Party's position is almost identical to that of the current Labour government, except that it has published a specific proposal intended to encourage people to save for their own old age while at the same time protecting their assets for a younger generation. Its proposal for a new long-term care savings fund[8] is a response to the concerns of homeowners and other more affluent groups. Even within the Labour Party, there are different views about the funding of long-term care, as is evident in Scotland, where the Scottish Executive is committed to introducing legislation making both nursing and personal care free.

Arriving at a satisfactory policy that commands widespread public and political support will not be easy. The tensions and dilemmas evident in current policy are deeply rooted in a health and welfare system that was designed more than 50 years ago. This system of long-term care was intended to sweep away the Poor Law, ending the indignities and deprivations experienced by older people reliant on public assistance institutions. But, as Robin Means shows, the decision then to distinguish between the sick elderly (with health care needs) and the elderly infirm (with social care needs) has caused difficulties ever since. Moreover, ambitions to improve the quality of care have been thwarted time and again as other priorities have predominated. Means argues that the legacy of the Poor Law can still be seen in the way long-term care is provided today. He suggests this indicates that deep-rooted negative attitudes towards ageing and towards older people as citizens have survived relatively intact.

Any debate about the merits and disadvantages of the current system of long-term care is almost invariably hampered by different understandings as to what the current policy actually is. At the heart of this confusion lie different perceptions concerning the social contract relating to care in old age. The concept of a social contract has long been used in welfare policy to refer to the terms and conditions by which governments will intervene on behalf of citizens. Equally, it indicates what citizens have to do to benefit from those interventions and what they can expect to happen in particular circumstances.

With long-term care, the contract is not clear. Few people recognise and understand what they have to do or what they can expect to happen. Many believe that recent governments have changed the contract without telling them. Thus, many older people and their carers believe they have been betrayed and that their rights have been infringed. They expected the Welfare State to look after them 'from cradle to grave'. A universal system of care free to all who fell ill would be provided by the National Health Service, financed by National Insurance contributions. The fact that this was not the case, as was evident in the 1948 National Assistance Act, is not the point. People believe that something has changed and that it is unfair that they should now be expected to pay for something they thought they had contributed to throughout their working lives. Among both older and younger generations, the rationale of a policy that rests on means-tested social care and free health care is, at the very least, questioned – if not opposed outright. This is perhaps most apparent in the logic that separates personal care from nursing care.[9]

The way in which long-term care policy evolved has led to a great deal of uncertainty among the general public about what elements of their own care they might have to pay for directly, what provision they should make for their own care, and what they can expect from government in terms of financial or other support. This same uncertainty raises questions about incentives to save, to purchase a house and to invest in a second pension, all of which can go some way to preparing for a comfortable old age but all of which may also be taken away as payment for long-term care. At the very least, greater clarity about the current social contract would help people to prepare for the future. It would also help to increase understanding of individuals' rights and responsibilities regarding the funding of long-term care.

Much of the current dissatisfaction with long-term care centres on arguments about rights. Recent governments have been reluctant to engage in a discourse about rights in social welfare. The heyday of rights-based policies was in the 1970s, when the Chronically Sick and Disabled Act 1971 gave disabled people rights to services when they had been assessed as being in need of them. The implementation of this Act has shown how limited resources dash the promise of substantive rights to care and support. Later governments, if they have focused on rights at all, have tended to concentrate on procedural rights that provide individuals with entitlements to be treated according to due process. Hence, in long-term care and, more generally, community care, much has been made of charters, complaints systems and so forth that are supposed to set out what people can expect to happen and which offer some recourse when things go wrong. Most recent examples have also laid out individuals' responsibilities, such as turning up for appointments or notifying those concerned if an appointment cannot be kept.

Unfortunately, this approach to rights and responsibilities obscures heated debates about the changing nature of welfare policy. Arguments about the end of universalism, the importance of targeting the most needy in society, about the residualisation of public services, are all based on particular notions of rights and responsibilities between the individual and the State. When it comes to long-term care, these arguments often reveal an assertion of rights that harks back to the founding of the Welfare State. This is certainly the case regarding those older people who feel betrayed by current long-term care policies. But it is equally true of others who put a high value on social solidarity and who, like Hilary Land, call for a return to a universalist policy.

Arguably, it is harder for Labour governments to confront these issues, given the attachment of the party and its supporters to the language of welfare that predominated at the time of the post-war settlement. However, given the confusion and uncertainty surrounding rights to long-term care, any new government – regardless of political hue – has a responsibility to lay out its vision of the social contract for the new century. Raymond Plant provides some thoughtful insights into the changing nature of the social contract and points to a way of achieving greater predictability in long-term care through hypothecated taxation for health and social care. But he also argues that whatever approach is adopted regarding rights to long-term care, there can be no unconditional, individually enforceable right to resources, nor any prospect of ending means-testing. He is clear that, whatever the philosophical and moral arguments, there can be no getting away from politics. Political judgements have to be made about the use of scarce resources and about the distribution of those resources. This makes it all the more important that governments make clear what package of care will be funded, and what that means in terms of personal and collective responsibility and the underpinning moral basis of these arrangements. It is only when they become more explicit that it will be possible to secure consent for a new social contract between citizen and State.

Support for the current system of funding long-term care is not strong. Indeed, it is widely regarded as being unfair. Yet, as Keen and Deeming indicate, current debates about long-term care entail competing notions of equity that are based on fundamental differences of philosophy. These different notions have not been spelt out and held up to public scrutiny. They argue that the Labour government's rhetoric makes much of equality and equity but, when it comes to long-term care funding, they attach greater importance to vertical equity, where those with greatest means contribute more resources, than to horizontal equity, where those with equal needs receive equal care. This contrasts with its position on funding the National Health Service, where the more affluent are not expected to pay more for their own health care (though they do contribute more to the *service as a whole* through a progressive taxation system). Government explanations about this policy preference have not been very convincing to pressure groups and public alike. Perhaps part of the reason for this is that the policy on long-term care does not appear to be located in any coherent philosophy regarding care and support in old age.

The future prospects for care in old age look worrying. All the signs are that increasing numbers of people are being expected to make more provision for their pensions and for long-term care. For some, like Land, the balance between public and private funding of care in old age has gone too far. She argues that the main losers will be people on low incomes and their carers, who will have to rely on inadequate public funding and residualised care services.

It appears that we have a system of long-term care funding that continues to be controversial and to be regarded as unsatisfactory in many different quarters. Creating something better will have to entail a conceptual leap that removes the untenable distinction between nursing and personal care, and sets long-term care squarely within the parameters of a national health service that supports people with acute and chronic conditions. But it will need to go wider than that, for care in old age is, as all contributors to this book acknowledge, closely related to other aspects of social policy – most notably pensions, welfare benefits associated with disability, housing, employment, and even transport. When the dust has settled on the new Health and Social Care Act, it will be time to examine afresh the way the different funding streams associated with care in old age operate and interact, with a view to creating a more coherent, equitable and efficient system for the rest of the twenty-first century. It might then be possible to say the Poor Law has at last been swept away for ever.

Chapter 2

Lessons from the history of long-term care for older people

Robin Means

Introduction

The Government is committed to a radical modernisation of health and welfare provision.[10,11] Long-term care, and the respective roles of the State and the individual, is an important component of this review, as evidenced by the establishment of the Royal Commission[12] and the subsequent response of the Government.[13]

Under these circumstances it is easy to dismiss the extent to which a knowledge of the past can throw light upon the problems and challenges of the present. This chapter draws upon two separate studies of the development of welfare services for older people[14,15] to argue that this would be a mistake. What is a fair and viable system of long-term care in old age has been a problem to confound politicians and policy-makers from the Poor Law onwards.

Part of the Royal Commission on Long Term Care's concern was to investigate:

- how best to fund long-term care
- whether or not a clear distinction could be made between health and social care
- which kind of environments, run by which kind of organisations, provide the best long-term care for older people.

All of these themes can be traced back to the Poor Law and post-war settlement. This chapter outlines how these debates have evolved and concludes by drawing out some of the conclusions regarding current concerns about the fairness and appropriateness of present long-term care policies.

From Poor Law to post-war settlement

By the 1930s, there was growing criticism of the Poor Law system, much of it by then administered by local authorities through large public assistance institutions (PAIs). The move to local authority control under the Local Government Act 1929 had left much of the old system intact so that 'poor law relief remained poor law relief and pauperism remained pauperism except for a few minor small modifications'.[16] Institutional regimes remained harsh, pension rights were lost and Elizabethan principles of family responsibility remained intact.

The need for reform was discussed at length at the 1937 Public Assistance Conference with encouragement from the Ministry of Health.[17] Olive Matthews was a noted campaigner for more interest to be brought into the lives of old people in institutions 'through contact with visitors from the outside world, by providing occupations as well as entertainments, and by introducing more variety into their food, clothing and surroundings'.[18] She was particularly influential in the passing of the Poor Law Amendment Act 1938, which gave local authorities a discretionary power to pay up to two shillings pocket money from the rates for each elderly person in their PAIs. Interestingly, this was opposed by the Association of Municipal Corporations on the grounds that it would be much better to remove the pension disqualifications rule. At the outbreak of the Second World War, there was a concern to improve the situation of elderly PAI residents, but this was not yet being couched by most people in terms of their rights as citizens.

The 1930s also saw growing uncertainty about the complex boundary between elderly people in poor law care for social reasons (and hence disqualified from pensions) and those in poor law infirmaries for health reasons (and hence still entitled to a pension). The establishment of municipal or public health hospitals accountable to public health committees rather than public assistance committees may have improved the overall quality of hospital-based health care, but it was at the expense of their growing reluctance to provide long-term health care for the elderly 'chronic sick'. There was a desperate national shortage of hospital beds for elderly people and considerable confusion about which elderly people needed to be in PAIs and which in Poor Law infirmaries. Large numbers of older people with long-term health and social care needs were, in reality, being 'housed' in PAIs, often confined to bed and with no attempt at rehabilitation.[19,20]

The Second World War, the reconstruction debate led by Beveridge in 1942, and the eventual post-war settlement were all to lead to a critical review of institutional provision for older people. Initially the impact of the war was calamitous for vast numbers of elderly people with long-term health and social care needs. Titmuss[21] outlines the various problems in the book he produced as part of the *Official history of the Second World War*: the war was disruptive of informal support networks; the establishment of the emergency medical service further reduced the availability of hospital beds; older people in those PAIs and Poor Law infirmaries at most risk of bombing raids were often not moved; elderly people in the larger cities struggled to cope with shelter life and were the group hardest hit by actual bomb damage to their homes.[22]

Evacuation schemes for older people were established, but these were often driven by a desire to reduce pressure upon and improve morale in communal air-raid shelters rather than being reflective of the complex needs of elderly evacuees:

> *Many did not want to be separated from their normal surroundings; married couples wanted to remain together; in some instances, the fear of being treated as a pauper was much more real than the fear of bombs. It became clear that the problem went far beyond the scope and resources of the emergency medical service. Not all the aged and*

> *infirm who were unable to stand the strain of shelter life were necessarily in need of hospital care. Many were still active enough to lead useful lives in more normal conditions. To confine them all indiscriminately to bed involved not only a waste of hospital resources but also the risk of making them permanently bedridden.*[23]

The alternative to bed, of course, was the PAI, but entry would 'brand' such war victims as paupers who would lose all pension rights. A campaign built up not only to 'humanise' PAIs but also to establish small homes and evacuation hostels outside of the PAI system for those whose lives had been disrupted by the war.[24]

An important influence on this debate was a letter entitled 'A Workhouse Visit' in the *Manchester Guardian* in March 1943. It described the living conditions of 'a frail, sensitive, refined old woman' of 84:

> *But down each side of the ward were ten beds, facing one another. Between each bed and its neighbour was a small locker and a straight-backed, wooden uncushioned chair. On each chair sat an old woman in a workhouse dress, upright, unoccupied. No library book or wireless. Central heating, but no open fire. No easy chairs. No pictures on the walls …There were three exceptions to the upright old women. None was allowed to lie on her bed at any time throughout the day, although breakfast is at 7 am, but these three, unable any longer to endure their physical and mental weariness, had crashed forward, face downwards, on to their immaculate bedspreads and were asleep.*[25]

The importance of the word 'refined' in the original description of the resident was, of course, to emphasise that this was a respectable person who deserved much better treatment at the end of her life.

The *Manchester Guardian* launched a campaign supported by the recently formed Old People's Welfare Committee (later Age

Concern), which caused the Ministry of Health to respond that workhouse clothes were no longer required and that 'the war has interrupted the early stages of substantial improvements in the care of old people ... but experiments in requisitioned country houses and evacuation hostels have brought valuable lessons for the future'.[26]

The Ministry supported the decision of the Nuffield Foundation, in the autumn of 1943, to establish a survey committee on the problems of ageing and the care of older people under the chairmanship of B S Rowntree. The subsequent report painted a picture of outdated institutions:

> *Floors are mainly bare boards, with brick floors in lavatories, bathrooms, kitchens and corridors. In large urban areas such institutions may accommodate as many as 1,500 residents of various types, including more than a thousand aged persons.[27]*

Many of these institutions continued to impose harsh rules and restrictions on freedom, with some staff allowing the cruel exploitation or neglect of older people. The report called for smaller homes, better-trained staff and a much greater emphasis upon liberty and the rights of older residents.

The situation of those elderly people with long-term health problems was especially severe, as confirmed by the parallel hospital surveys that took place in the same period:

> *All are agreed that the reproach of the masses of undiagnosed and untreated cases of chronic type which litter our Public Assistance Institutions must be removed. Without proper classification and investigation, at present young children and senile dements are 'banded together' in these institutions, along with many elderly patients whom earlier diagnosis and treatment might have enabled to return to their homes ... The great essential is that every patient should be thoroughly examined and treated with a view to restoration*

to a maximum degree of activity. Only if treatment is unsuccessful or is clearly useless, should [he] be regarded as chronically sick, and even then [he] should be subject to a periodic review.[28]

The main recommendation was that elderly people with health care needs required to be completely divorced from arrangements to support those with social care needs.

The post-war settlement did include major change in attitudes to older people and in how this was expressed through provision. The National Health Service Act 1946 brought together the different strands of hospital provision within a single free service and thus, in theory at least, overcame the previous problem of health discrimination against older people. Certainly, this period embraced a greater optimism about the ability to meet such need and to do this in a way committed to active rehabilitation.[29] However, it was a perspective based upon a belief that it was possible to distinguish between the health care needs of the 'elderly sick' and the welfare needs of the 'elderly infirm'.

How best to respond to the needs of the latter group was also reviewed in the same period. The Government established a committee under Sir Arthur Rucker to advise on the break up of the Poor Law. First, this confirmed that institutions for this group should continue to be run by local authorities but that the focus should switch to the provision of small homes. Second, the committee considered a number of issues related to funding. Its report called for a standard fee structure and recommended that the old system of extensive familial responsibility should be swept away and replaced with a simple liability of spouses in respect of each other. The old system of pension disqualifications was also to go:

...as a further step towards breaking away from the old association of parish relief and in particular the conception of an institution for 'destitute persons', we think that a resident in a local authority's

Home should keep charge of whatever income or other resources he may have and pay the authority for his accommodation and maintenance.[30]

The proposed model was that 21 shillings per week of the new 26 shillings pension would be a minimum contribution by all elderly residents to their board, with five shillings retained for what was called 'pocket money'. However, the proposed new system was to take a tough line on savings and capital assets:

> *It may reasonably be argued that an old person who has no family to look after him or whose family are freed by his entering the institution from the trouble of caring for him, should be expected to use any capital he has (and to realise it where it is invested, e.g. in house property) to meet the standard charge for so long as the capital will enable him to do so.*[31]

Thus, the belief that home equity should be used to help fund the costs of residential-based social care but not hospital or nursing home health care has much longer roots than most people appreciate.

The main recommendations of the Rucker Report were incorporated into the National Assistance Act 1948. The then Minister of Health, Nye Bevan, spoke of the need to develop 30-bed homes for 'the type of old person who is still able to look after themselves ... but who is unable to do the housework, the laundry, cook meals and things of that sort'.[32] He felt elderly people would pay an economic rent and so would be able to 'go there in exactly the same way as many well-to-do people have been accustomed to go into residential hotels'.[33]

The local authority residential home was to be available to all those the Act defined as being 'in need of care and attention' and initial hopes were high:

The old institutions or workhouses are to go altogether. In their place will be attractive hostels or hotels, each accommodating 25 to 30 old people, who will live there as guests not inmates. Each guest will pay for his accommodation – those with private income out of that, those without private income out of the payments they get from the National Assistance Board – and nobody need know whether they have private means or not. Thus, the stigma of 'relief' – very real too, and acutely felt by many old people – will vanish at last.[34]

The reality proved to be much more problematic.

What is health care? What is social care? Welfare provision for older people, 1948–71

In the period up to their replacement by unified social services authorities in April 1971, welfare authorities struggled to deliver the new aspirations. Some smaller homes were created through the conversion of large country houses, but the bulk of provision remained in the large Victorian institutions so condemned in the Rowntree Report. It was not until 1960 that the number of new-build residential homes per year passed 30[35] and as a result the survey of residential homes by Townsend[36] in the early 1960s made depressingly familiar reading. Much of this elderly accommodation had further deteriorated, multi-occupancy of rooms was the norm, and basic amenities such as hand basins, toilets and baths were not only insufficient but were often difficult to reach, badly distributed and of poor quality. Ministry of Health reports[37] were admitting that 'local authorities have been reluctant to incur expenditure on old premises that they hoped soon to relinquish'. Other research highlighted that many of the converted homes were completely unsuited for use as residential homes because of their geographical isolation and poor access standards.[38]

Townsend discovered that the staffing situation was little better. Most staff had been simply transferred from the Poor Law administration with no re-training and so:

...it would be idle to pretend that many of them were imbued with the more progressive standards of personal care encouraged by the Ministry of Health ... A minority of them were unsuitable, by any standards, for the tasks they performed, men or women with authoritarian attitudes inherited from Poor Law days who provoked resentment or even terror among infirm people.[39]

Such circumstances made the idea of a hotel relationship completely unrealistic. However, this was also true because the overall shortage of residential care home beds meant that it became necessary to assess more clearly what was meant by being 'in need of care and attention'. This proved incredibly difficult because the Act and accompanying circulars gave no clear guidance on the boundary between social care and health care. Hospitals were seeking to discharge large numbers of elderly people into residential homes – local authorities felt many of these people still had health care rather than social care needs.

Godlove and Mann[40] have argued that 'the authors ... of this Act ... did not envisage this type of care as being adequate for people suffering from incontinence, serious loss of mobility, or abnormal senile dementia'. From this perspective, the problem was that local authority residential homes contained large numbers of elderly people in need of hospital care.[41] Against this, hospital boards were expressing frustration at bed blockages as a result of their inability to discharge elderly people into such provision. The main area of agreement was about the existence of a group of elderly people who were 'stranded in the no man's land between the Regional Hospital Board and the local welfare department – not ill enough for one, not well enough for the other'.[42] The 1950s saw numerous attempts to establish rest homes or halfway houses to meet the specific needs of this group.[43]

The response of government was to commission the Boucher Report[44] into health and welfare provision in later life:

The number of beds for the chronic sick in England and Wales is thought to be about sufficient in total if they are properly used and better distributed. The efficient use depends on the strength of the rehabilitation services, the sufficiency of welfare accommodation for the infirm, and the adequacy of the local health services and of the voluntary services.

However, 4500 patients in 'chronic sick' wards were considered no longer to need hospital care but were unable to move on because of the lack of ground floor accommodation/lifts in local authority residential care.

What it meant to be 'in need of care and attention' was in the process of being redefined. As a result of the Boucher Inquiry, circulars were issued to both local authorities and to hospital authorities about their respective responsibilities. Welfare authorities were informed that their duties included:

- *care of the otherwise active resident in a welfare home during minor illness which may well involve a short period in bed;*
- *care of the infirm (including the senile) who may need help in dressing, toilet, etc, and may need to live on the ground floor because they cannot manage stairs, and may spend part of the day in bed (or longer periods in bad weather);*
- *care of those elderly persons in a welfare home who have to take to bed and are not expected to live more than a few weeks (or exceptionally months) and who would, if in their own homes, stay there because they cannot benefit from treatment or nursing care beyond help that can be given at home, and whose removal to hospital away from their familiar surroundings and attendants would be felt to be inhumane.*[45]

Hospital authorities, on the other hand, were expected to take responsibility for:

- *care of the chronic bedfast who may need little or no medical treatment but do require prolonged nursing care over months or years;*

- *convalescent care of the elderly sick who have completed active treatment but who are not yet ready for discharge to their own homes or to welfare homes;*
- *care of senile confused or disturbed patients who are, owing to their mental condition, unfit to live a normal community life in a welfare home.*[46]

Hospital authorities did not have responsibility to give 'all medical or nursing care needed by an old person, however minor the illness or however short the stay in bed, nor to admit all those who need nursing care because they are entering on the last stage of their lives'.

The circulars were giving a clear steer about the need to re-interpret what was meant by 'in need of care and attention', yet they were still riddled with interpretation problems. How easy was it to know when a bedfast patient would die? Was there a clear distinction between the senile and senile confused? At what point did spending significant time in bed cause you to be labelled bedfast? The circulars became the basis of bargaining over individual cases between health and social services in which 'the swap'[47] developed, where many hospitals refused to accept a referral from a residential home unless that home (or another in the local authority) would accept a patient from a geriatric unit of the hospital. Elderly people had few rights in this situation and it is likely that many continued to be moved around the various kinds of institutional care, according to the balance of power between the various professionals involved.

The 1957 circulars were updated in 1965, with an ever stronger emphasis upon the high level of dependency through frailty and ill health that a residential home should be able to cope with:

The elderly people whom (they) may need to admit or to retain in homes can broadly be described as those who are found, after careful assessment of their medical and social needs, to be unable to maintain themselves in their own homes, even with full support from outside, but who do not need continuous care by nursing staff. They include:

> i) *people so incapacitated that they need help with dressing, toilet and meals but who are able to get about with a walking aid or with some help by wheelchair;*
>
> ii) *people using appliances that they can manage themselves or without nursing assistance;*
>
> ii) *people with temporary or continuing confusion of mind but who do not need psychiatric nursing care.*
>
> *They include also residents who fall ill, whether for short or long periods, whose needs are no greater than could be met in their own homes by relatives with the aid of the local health services. Where the illness is expected to be terminal, transfer to hospital should be avoided unless continuous medical or nursing care is necessary. Some incontinent residents (other than those with intractable incontinence and other disabilities) may also be manageable in a residential home.*[48]

Local authority residential care had become 'home' to a very different group of people to that envisaged by Rucker, Bevan and others. Attempts to clarify the boundary between health and social care had drawn into local authority care a group who had once been seen as clearly having health care needs that should be responded to free of charge through the health service.

Towards marketisation, 1971–93*

The economic and political context of this period was one of initial growth in the public sector under a Conservative government, which generated a major expansion of local authority residential care followed by economic cutbacks and retrenchment under a number of different Conservative and Labour governments. Such an environment was always likely to further foster tension over the boundaries between health and social care. The extent of this has been illustrated by service developments from 1971 to 1993 in two county councils, a metropolitan authority and a London borough.[49]

---

* This section draws upon research funded by ESRC (Grant no. R000 23 7279).

The London borough commissioned a survey of the dependency levels of its residential home residents in 1975. This covered 483 older people living in ten homes, and discovered that one in five needed help moving between rooms, one in nine was doubly incontinent, significant numbers were either somewhat or severely confused and that considerable staff time was being consumed in overseeing the taking of drugs and providing basic nursing care. The local authority felt it required much greater support from the health service but was told by a representative of the area health authority that there was a failure to grasp the changing notion of nursing care. More specifically, 'nursing was now considered as that part of the service which required very specialised skills rather than simply caring'.[*]

Similar examples are to be found in the other three case studies. For example, one of the two county councils complained that:

> Reference to Part III accommodation currently providing some type of nursing home care graphically highlights the problems which are currently falling on the Social Services Department by providing services which are inappropriate to their skills and resources. These pressures will continue, and the Department and its staff will need to take great care that inappropriate burdens are not passed to them.[†]

The Metropolitan authority shared these concerns and felt that 'for much of the time in many of the homes, all staff can do is look after the physical needs of residents, ignoring their social and emotional needs'.[‡]

---

[*] Social Services Committee (Metropolitan Authority). *Dependency levels of residents in council homes for the elderly.* 8 December 1975.

[†] Social Services Committee (County Council A). *Area health authority – creation of first Health Area Plan.* 18 March 1977.

[‡] Social Services Committee (Metropolitan Authority). *Staffing in residential establishments.* 6 June 1978.

Conflict over this issue rumbled on well into the 1980s, and joint finance was often used to tackle this problem. One frequent outcome was the development of newly built residential homes designed and staffed to provide a service for older people with dementia or others with high dependency needs. However, such homes proved expensive, and too often led to disputes about how they did or did not relate to NHS provision and to the rest of local authority residential care. With the spectacular growth of private sector homes during the 1980s, these experiments were often abandoned.

Under Margaret Thatcher, the Conservative government of 1979 came to power with a mission to cut back the Welfare State and to reduce public expenditure. Ironically, one of the policy changes in long-term care led to an explosion in the private residential and nursing home sector caused by changes in the social security system. Supplementary Benefit regulations were amended in the early 1980s and this made it much easier for the residents of independent sector homes to claim their fees from social security. Provision in this sector mushroomed from 49,900 places in 1982 to 161,200 places in 1991.[50] Social security expenditure rose from £10 million in 1979 to £459 million in 1986 and a staggering £2,575 million in 1993.[51]

These major developments had a lasting impact on the balance of responsibilities between the individual and the State. First, the health service was able to use the growth of private nursing homes to rapidly reduce the availability of NHS beds for the chronic sick (now called 'continuing care'). Rather than being in free NHS care, many older people found themselves in private nursing homes facing a means test, which involved a consideration of their capital assets, including their housing wealth. The inheritance implications for the next generation were considerable and became an issue of some political saliency.

Second, even though 'rights' to free health care appeared to have been withdrawn, older people seemed to have finally been offered the hotel option outlined by Bevan in the mid-1940s. In most areas of the country there was a growing availability of independent sector residential and nursing homes. Older people could enter these without any assessment of their need for such expensive care and they could immediately access social security monies to support such care if they were on low incomes with limited capital assets. A market in institutional care was created but one fuelled by a massive public subsidy. Such a situation could not continue and the community care reform elements of the NHS and Community Act 1990 were seen by most commentators as driven by the need to 'cap' this rapidly increasing expenditure.[52]

The rapid development of the private residential and nursing home sector only served to increase tensions around local authority residential care. From the mid-1970s onwards, there was only limited investment in buildings and very little thought about regimes, to a point where one might wonder at how little progress had been made since the days of Olive Matthews. Thus, the Social Services Committee of the London borough received the following report about one if its homes in 1975:

> ... one very large room on the ground floor has been divided into two. Six gentlemen sleep in one half, seven gentlemen in the other. The ceiling is high; adding to the institutional feeling of the room, but the main cause for concern is the overcrowding and subsequent lack of any possibility of privacy. The beds have to be set side by side and are separated by a space of less than three feet, that space being taken up by a locker.*

Nearly all homes in the four case studies were experiencing the consequences of a lack of investment in repairs and modernisation. This was brutally exposed by the standards expected of the independent sector through the adoption of the code of practice, *Home life*.[53] Local authorities were faced with a stark choice. They could seek to close the most outdated homes and transfer the remaining stock out of local authority control (which it was hoped

---

* Social Services Committee (Metropolitan Authority). *Occupancy of homes for the elderly: proposed reduction in places available*. 8 December 1975.

would release funds to invest in community-based services), or they could attempt to fund a major capital re-investment programme. Thus, one of the county councils had estimated the need for a £10.8 million refurbishment programme for 12 homes in 1992 (two homes to be upgraded per year) when it already had an estimated capital shortfall of £8 million for 1995/96.* The former chair of the Social Services Committee of the second county council remembered there being 'a ball park figure in the early 1990s of around £11 to £12 million' to bring the local authority residential homes 'up to scratch'.†

Social services authorities found it very difficult to resolve these tensions. The money for mass refurbishment was not available, yet residents, many councillors and much of the general public were against closure or even home transfer. The end result was what one Director of Social Services called 'EPH wars'.[54]

Discussion

This chapter has illustrated the incredibly long roots of the debate about what represents a fair deal in old age with regard to long-term care. This look at the history of such provision from the Poor Law through to the early 1990s has illustrated a number of critical points.

The Poor Law legacy

Both residential care and continuing health care have found it incredibly difficult to shake off the legacy of the Poor Law. Poor-quality buildings run by low-morale staff seem so often to have been the experience of older people with long-term care needs, and a sense of stigma is still attached to residential care. The ability of this Poor Law legacy to linger so long is surely reflective of broader ageist attitudes in society.[55] The NHS Plan, including the Government's

---

*   Social Services Committee (County Council A). *Services for elderly people – home refurbishment standard.* 3 March 1992.

†   Interview with chair of Social Services Committee (County Council B).

response to the Royal Commission on Long Term Care, offers the possibility of new beginnings that finally lay to rest this past history of neglect. However, some real dangers need to be recognised. The emphasis upon intermediate care and rehabilitation is admirable, but the spirit of its implementation will be crucial. We could see a blossoming of hospital-at-home schemes, rapid response teams and community rehabilitation teams. However, an emphasis on an end to bed blocking in NHS hospitals could encourage the inappropriate use of residential and nursing homes to warehouse older people under the guise of intermediate care.

Who should pay?

The National Assistance Act 1948 was an attempt to strike a balance between the responsibilities of the individual and the State in terms of meeting the costs of residential care, and through this mechanism destroy the old concept of destitution and pauperism. Older people would be paying their way, though with extensive public subsidies based upon general taxation.

However, continuing health care was initially seen as part of the health service and so free to the individual at the point of use. Concerns about the costs to the health service of elderly people have long encouraged governments and health authorities to 'push' ever-more dependent elderly people into the responsibility of local authorities. The alternative strategy that developed in the mid-1980s was directing older people to private nursing homes where most of their care costs would be met through the social security system rather than the budget of the National Health Service.

Back in 1946, little note was taken of the Rucker Report's proposals on capital assets and housing wealth for those in local authority residential care. Most elderly people had few such assets, mainly because their homes were much more likely to be rented than owned. More than 50 years on, the situation is transformed, with Britain now 'a nation of home owners',[56] including many older people.[57] And the use of home equity is expected of those in independent sector nursing homes as well as those in all forms of residential care. The exception remains the ever-reducing minority of older people in long-term NHS continuing care, since they are not subject to the same means test of their income and assets.

This illogical situation was one of the main reasons why the Sutherland Report argued that health and welfare provision to meet long-term needs in later life should be paid for through general taxation and free at the point of consumption.

What is health care? What is social care?

This chapter has shown without doubt that the boundaries between health and social care are constantly shifting and open to renegotiation. They have been an endless source of tension and conflict between local authorities and health authorities. The NHS Plan seems to recognise this through its proposals to bring health and social services together in care trusts. However, it seems to re-assert the existence of this distinction in its response to the Royal Commission – the nursing component of nursing home care is to be free, but 'social care' in residential homes will continue to be means-tested and charged for. The historical perspective offered in this chapter suggests that it will prove extremely difficult to make this distinction 'stick'. Is it not time to finally accept that no sensible separation can be made between the health and welfare elements of the long-term support needs of older people?

New visions and economic imperatives

The history of long-term care reveals some genuine attempts to create a new vision for residential and nursing home care, with the hotel concept being the most obvious example. Too often such aspirations have been undermined by economic and affordability concerns. The small residential homes required of the 1948 Act were never built.

The Royal Commission proposed a vision in which all personal care would be free for those assessed as being in need of such support. It is hard to avoid the conclusion that economic concerns have driven the negative response of the Government. Older people in the twenty-first century deserve much better than this and it is to be hoped that a new government will carry out a further review of long-term care.

Chapter 3

Rights and responsibilities in long-term care

Raymond Plant

The changing Welfare State

The scope and the funding of long-term care for elderly people has become a central issue in social policy. It raises a number of complex theoretical questions about the nature of the contract between the State and the citizen, in terms of what the citizen can reasonably expect from the State and what the State in its turn can reasonably regard as matters of personal rather than collective responsibility. Long-term care has to be seen in the context of a Welfare State that has been characterised since the late 1970s by a weakening of the idea of a 'cradle to grave' Welfare State, providing resources that many of those who are now elderly or approaching old age expected to be in place when they needed them. The role of the State *vis-à-vis* the market and community has been changing, although this revision has been highly incremental. In the case of long-term care, it has also been rather indirect in that it was only from the 1970s that the NHS began to divest itself of responsibilities it had hitherto assumed in relation to the care of elderly people. This has meant that we have reached the point at which long-term care policy decisions are being made without the population at large being fully prepared for such changes and without a full understanding of their implications and consequences.

It is now imperative for government to make clear not only which package of care will in fact be funded (which it has done), but also which assumptions have to be made about personal versus collective responsibility and on which moral basis each of these features rests. Only when we are much more explicit about these underlying assumptions will it be possible to secure consent for a new contract between State and citizen. This would bring to bear new views about the responsibilities of government, the individual and the community, and with these the role of the market in relation to private insurance for a range of welfare goods and the voluntary sector in relation to the delivery of social policy goals.

The modern Welfare State was put in place after the Second World War, but it had been preceded by the Beveridge Report, which had set out its account of the relationship between State, citizen and community in a free society. This formed the basis of the post-1945 welfare settlement that was accepted by all political parties. It was also underpinned by a high degree of social solidarity, which had been engendered partly by the country becoming a 'community of fate' during the war years and partly by the collective memory of the 1930s and a determination not to go back to the social and economic policies of that period. Obviously, circumstances today are very different.

Whatever the virtues (and they are many) of the Sutherland Commission, it was required to focus on one welfare issue – long-term care. Unlike Beveridge, the Commission was not able to consider the full range of issues necessary to arrive at a more synoptic and systematic view of the complex nature of a new welfare settlement covering social security, the health service and welfare. Without this broader perspective, it is quite difficult to argue for a new contract in one aspect of welfare, such as long-term care, while actually hanging on to principles and policies in other areas of the Welfare State that are in fact rejected in relation to long-term care. This piecemeal approach makes it much more difficult to devise a moral framework that could be regarded as underpinning a new relationship between public and private, collective and individual responsibility in relation to long-term care, just because issues of this sort pervade the Welfare State and are quite likely to have to be tackled in other spheres, particularly health care. So, instead of a unifying vision of the relationship between welfare and citizenship that Beveridge provided, we have a much more fragmented approach. In this context, consent will be sought by governments for seemingly small changes in policy, but the incremental effect may be a result that few would choose had they the opportunity to confront the issues in the round.

Principles and policies

It is equally difficult to produce a set of normative principles that could be seen as an authoritative guide in relation to long-term care. There is no moral Archimedian point that can determine policies; even if there were, general principles invariably under-determine policies. Indeed, the members of the Sutherland Commission actually agreed on a set of moral principles, but this did not stop Lords Lipsey and Joffe drawing conclusions in their minority report that ran counter to a central thrust in the main report. Nor is there one moral perspective that can be regarded as fully authoritative. Rather, there is a number of what might be thought of as normative models. It would, however, be false to think that we have a neutral set of objective criteria that could be used to assess these different models and which could yield a single verdict concerning the most effective or most compelling model. The criteria of assessment are themselves disputable.

This chapter examines several of these models that define in different ways the scope of collective provision of welfare goods such as long-term care for the elderly and which have different funding implications and different calls upon public and private types of funding. I shall distinguish two alternative models, within which there are further alternatives available.

Rights-based approaches to long-term care

(a) Long-term care paid for as a right of citizenship, payable unconditionally by virtue of the status of citizenship and funded out of taxation. This is the model of a contract between citizen and State that many, who now feel badly let down, have in mind.

It forms the underlying moral basis for their claim that their legitimate expectations have not been met and that it is this form of contract that has been so eroded over the past 25 years.

(b) An insurance model, in which the risks associated with the need for long-term care can be pooled and resources provided as a right grounded in the contributory principle via an insurance system. Theoretically this could be a system that is either: 1) a State system; 2) a private system but with a legal requirement to pay into it; or 3) a private system without compulsory participation.

In a sense, the erosion of the prevailing system has been resented because people felt that they had a right to the care based either on a contribution via the tax system or via National Insurance. In both cases there is an assumption that there is a right to the care because it has been paid for through one or other of these contributory systems.

Model (a) depends upon a very strong view of citizenship in respect of rights, needs and universality. The core assumption here is that the status of being a citizen entails that various basic needs and interests that all citizens share in common should be mutually recognised. There is also an acceptance that these needs/interests can in fact only be protected by a collective system and that only a collective system can manage to avoid the vulnerability of particular individuals who might be exposed to unforeseen and sometimes catastrophic situations. Given that these are universal needs and contingencies in a particular society, it is argued that the satisfaction and protection of these needs and interests should be met out of general taxation and that there is a right to such satisfaction and protection.

Negative and positive rights

These needs and interests can be seen as both negative and positive. Negative interests would involve an interest in being free from coercion, assault, manipulation, invasion of privacy, etc; positive interests relate to health, education and security. In both cases, these interests and the needs on which they are based are so fundamental that they can be regarded as rights and that collective protection of such rights is basic to citizenship. As forms of protection collectively provided, justified on the basis of the common status of citizenship, such protection should be funded out of general taxation. It could be argued that there is an exact parallel to be drawn with the provision of the police and courts to protect our universal interest in having our negative rights protected, with the provision for our equally basic interests in and need for certain kinds of welfare goods.

As I have already said, it seems fairly clear from the sense of betrayal that many people now feel that they did hold, in however an implicit manner, to some such conception of the role of citizenship, taxation and collective provision. This position has, however, come under very severe criticism over the past 25 years or so and it is important to understand why.

First of all, critics argue that there is no clear symmetry between negative sorts of rights – to be left alone and to be free from coercion – and positive rights to resources of various sorts, such as care in old age. The reason for this has to do with scarcity. A right not to be harmed does not require the commitment of resources in the way that a right to care in old age does. The duty of others in respect of my right not to be harmed is to abstain from harming me – that is a negative duty: it involves not acting. The duties that a recognition of my negative rights lay on others are costless and are not subject to scarcity. We cannot run out of people not harming one another. The opposite is true for positive rights such as the right to care – it is intrinsically a right to the provision of resources. As such it is subject to scarcity and hence rationing and discretion. On this view there cannot be an individually enforceable right to such care. To countenance such rights would lead to a completely open-ended commitment to the provision of resources on the part of government in each particular area of the Welfare State in which those rights were asserted.

It might be argued that the distinction between negative and positive rights has been drawn too sharply in respect of scarcity and the difference between the corresponding duties. Negative rights to non-interference also necessarily involve resources. The reasons here are twofold – one practical, the other philosophical. The practical reason is that in fact people do interfere, harm and coerce, and they have to be prevented from so doing by the police, the courts and so forth. So, in practice the protection of the right to be free from coercion is going to involve resources and thus be subject to the same constraints about scarcity as positive rights. The philosophical reason is more theoretical. It is based on the idea that a right is only a right if it can be enforced. We have all sorts of needs and interests, only some of which are turned into rights. Those that are regarded as giving rise to rights are so regarded partly because of their fundamental importance in human life and also because it makes sense to think that they can be enforced. So, for example, our need for love may be absolutely basic to our lives, but of course it makes no sense to turn it into a right because it is not the sort of thing that can be enforced without destroying precisely what our need is for. The enforceability of a right is what makes a right a right. However, the enforceability conditions of a right necessarily involve resources and will thus run up against scarcity considerations. In this respect, the right to the protection of negative rights is itself a positive right.

Nevertheless, while it could be argued that all rights involve a right to the protection of rights and that this protection will have to be provided collectively and funded out of general taxation, paradoxically this does not yield an unconditional, individually enforceable right to that protection because of the scarcity problem. All the above argument does in the view of the critic is to generalise to negative rights the problem of scarcity that applies intrinsically to positive rights. So, for example, the problem of scarcity in health care means that there cannot be an individually enforceable right to the services of a surgeon or any other health procedure. Limited resources mean that discretion has to be exercised in terms of how these resources will be distributed to individuals and that this is not compatible with individual rights in the sense that rights are individually enforceable. The same is true of the police force: while a chief constable has a duty to maintain his/her force and to investigate all sorts of crime and not, as a matter of policy, neglect crime of a particular character, this does not yield an individually enforceable right to the services of a police officer. The reason for this is obvious: if all rights involve resources and an individually enforceable right to those resources, then the cost to the State in terms of the protection of such rights would be astronomical and completely open-ended. Given that they would, on the purist view, be provided free of charge and on the basis of equality of access, then the demand for such resources might well be infinite, given the rather unspecified nature of the content of the rights being claimed.

The right to fair shares

The defender of a rights-oriented view of a tax-funded right to long-term care might at this point argue as follows. Clearly there cannot be a right to unlimited resources either for a particular individual or for the care budget as a whole. So, the idea of a right has to be linked to the idea of social justice. Here, the right would not be to an unlimited set of resources so much as a just or fair share of a set of finite resources. So, the idea of rights has to be linked to the idea of social justice and to non-discrimination. However, once this line of argument is followed it immediately produces a wide range of further complexities to do with the nature and significance of the idea of social justice. The first thing to be said about social justice is that there is no single authoritative account of its nature and its demands. There might be all sorts of incompatible criteria in terms of which goods could be distributed and each of these distributions could be regarded as just. So, for example, a good could be distributed in terms of need, of merit or desert, of equality, of entitlement, or of contribution. The invocation of one of these criteria will lead to a different distribution compared with another criterion, and there is no authoritative way in which these issues can be resolved.

It might, of course, be argued that justice should be seen as complex and that a full theory of justice should find a place for ideas like need, equality and desert. While this is an attractive idea, it is fatally flawed because we have no way of ranking these criteria against one another: when do we stop meeting needs and move on to merit or contribution? These judgements have to become political. They cannot be read off some kind of moral template or derived from the idea of rights themselves.

They also cannot be derived from the nature of the goods to be distributed.[58] We cannot, by fixing our attention on the long-term care needs of elderly people, produce some kind of non-political account of the nature of the goods that will satisfy these needs and derive an idea of a just form of funding based upon these goods. As the Sutherland Report makes clear, there are different components of the goods to meet these needs: personal care, nursing care, accommodation costs, etc. There is nothing intrinsic to these goods that will enable us to figure out in a theoretical way how they should be distributed. It cannot just be that we see them as basic needs because there are needs that are quite fundamental to us but which, by and large, we leave to market mechanisms rather than to collective provision – food would be a good example. How basic goods should be produced and distributed cannot be determined just by the nature of the goods themselves: this has to be done through political debate and dialogue.

The link between rights and social justice is very important because the very pluralism and indeed incommensurability of different criteria of social justice, ranging from need to contribution, opens up the debate about the relative salience of such criteria in relation to the collective provision of long-term care. This leads us into a situation in which we have to accept that there can be contending criteria of just distribution and a role for different views about what should be met unconditionally and what should be met via personal contribution. There is no way of reading off the answers to these questions just by asserting that there is a clear right to collective provision. Therefore, although it may have seemed to be the case that there could be a secure right in terms of citizenship to long-term care, this cannot be so as it stands. A claim to such a right has to be linked to a defence of a particular view of what it is just to expect society to pay for, and this will be a highly contested and political matter.

It is worth pointing out an obvious point at this stage: namely, that the tax funding underpinning a citizenship approach would be on a pay-as-you-go basis. It would in no sense be a funded scheme. Rather, the present generation of taxpayers pays for the long-term care of the previous generation and that present generation in its turn would expect to be paid for by its children's generation. The citizenship approach, therefore, depends upon an intergenerational contract and, since we are currently coming to long-term decisions, the effect of these decisions may assume a degree of intergenerational reciprocity in terms of future generations of taxpayers as yet unborn. It might be thought that this fact should give us pause for reflection. It might seem that, if a citizenship approach depends upon intergenerational solidarity, we have to be modest rather than maximalist in terms of what we expect future generations to pay for. Or, more radically, that we should abandon the citizenship/rights-based/unconditional approach that has to depend on pay-as-you-go in favour of a funded scheme based on a contributory and insurance mechanism

There are two further points to be made about the rights-based/tax-funded approach, which will usefully lead us to the next model based upon the idea of insurance. The first point, made frequently by Frank Field (former Minister for Welfare Reform), is that citizenship and the rights of citizenship constitute far too abstract a set of moral conceptions in terms of which to ground consent to a welfare regime. Rather, the link has to be far closer to people's experience in everyday life. This point then leads into the second one: namely, that citizenship is too abstract a conception, for people might believe that they have genuine claims on social resources. This point has been made very well by Robert Pinker:

The idea of paying through taxes or holding authentic claims by virtue of citizenship remains largely an intellectual conceit of the social scientist and the socialist. For the majority the idea of participant citizenship in distributive processes outside the market place has very little meaning.[59]

On this view two things follow. The first is that it is a mistake to believe that citizenship gives rise to unconditional rights. The second, following from the first, is that it would be a mistake to interpret the sense of betrayal that people have at the moment as being the result of a perceived infringement of their citizens' rights. If Pinker is correct, very few will have held such views in the past. Rather, the answer is to be found in insurance.

Rights through insurance contributions

Insurance can yield genuine rights because it is part of a contract and the recipient of the benefit has paid for the pooling of a risk and, at the appropriate time, he/she can claim a right that is basically contractual. On this view, the betrayal should be seen in relation to the idea that National Insurance, rather than general taxation, was to pay for long-term care and that individuals had secured an insurance-based right to care through paying NI contributions. Second, it would also follow that the solution to the idea of a right to care in old age should be linked to a revamped insurance system rather than a tax-funded right of citizenship. Thus, the underlying idea here is that a right arises out of a contract, in this case an insurance contract, and not from an abstract status.

Supporters of an insurance-based approach to these issues argue that such an approach avoids the judgements about distributive justice that have to be invoked in relation to collectively provided tax-funded schemes. It also eliminates the role of discretion that is bound to arise in relation to collective resources where there are no clearly agreed and detailed criteria of distribution. It also avoids means-testing, which is always likely to arise in relation to tax-funded welfare schemes. Essentially you get what you pay for and you have a right to what you have paid to insure yourself against. Insurance-based approaches can be either private or public, like the National Insurance contribution. However, as we shall see, the insurance-based approach produces almost exactly the same sorts of difficulties as the tax-based perspective, which we have already discussed.

These difficulties are evident in the private insurance scheme proposed to the Sutherland Commission by Patrick Minford, whose views would be widely echoed among neo-liberal and New Right economists. On this view, an individual pays an insurance premium that will cover the risks set out in the policy. He or she then has a right to the resources when circumstances arise that fit the terms of the policy. It is argued that there are no disputes about resource distribution, no discretion and no means-testing. However, this is clearly not the case. First of all, it is highly unlikely that all members of the population would in fact choose to take out private insurance. Large numbers of people will have to pay for private care out of income and capital and they may not have the resources to do so if their need for care is long term. The question then is whether the State would step in to pick up the bill out of general taxation for those who had expected (wrongly) to be able to meet the costs of care themselves. Second, there are also those who do not have the resources to pay the costs of the insurance premiums or who may in fact be bad risks. In these circumstances, again, there would be a question of whether the State would step in to pick up the bill or to pay the premiums of people in these sorts of positions.

The important point, however, is that both of these sets of circumstances raise questions about collective provision and distributive justice, and no doubt also discretion and means-testing. Questions of justice arise in relation to the extent to which it is just to use tax revenues to fund people whose expectations have turned out to be false and when they have not, in the light of those expectations, made provision for themselves. Apart from the general issue of justice here, there is also the matter of discretion. Government bureaucracies would have to determine which individual cases were deserving and which were not. It would also include means-testing, because individuals would otherwise have an incentive to exaggerate the degree of need. In addition, there would be a question about the standards of citizenship that the insurance-based approach was thought to bypass, since there would be the question of whether the State should provide resources for care at a residual level for those who had mistaken their capacity to look after themselves. The difficulty here is that if the State funded such people at the same level as those covered by insurance, there would be a strong moral hazard – giving people an incentive not to insure since they would get the same benefits if their own funds did not cover them for care.

Exactly the same moral problems in respect of collective provision would arise in these circumstances as arise in relation to a tax-funded system. This also applies to the issue of future generations. On a pay-as-you-go private insurance system, the present generation of taxpayers would have to fund the previous generation insofar as they had made mistakes about what their own resources would be likely to underpin.

The identical issues arise in relation to the position of those who would be too poor to afford premiums for private insurance. Questions of justice, discretion and means-testing would certainly rise in relation to whether or not individuals were clearly unable to afford insurance provision; and the cut-off point would be fairly arbitrary and wherever it came it would be required to be subject to means-testing. So, the private insurance approach, if based on the principle of voluntary choice, may avoid the problems of justice, discretion and means-testing for those within the circle of insurance, but exactly the same problems would be encountered for those outside it. Either the State would have to step in with provision for the worst off or it would have to credit the poor into private insurance schemes and this would involve basic questions about discretion, cut-off points, perverse incentives and distributive justice.

Hence, unless one buys into the whole libertarian package[60] (which would say that the State should not step in to rescue those who have made mistakes in estimating their own capacity to look after themselves or who have always been too poor to cover the costs of insurance and that their situation should be dealt with by private charity), it is difficult to see how a voluntary private insurance scheme can sidestep the same sorts of moral difficulties as apply to tax-funded long-term care. Indeed, as I have suggested, tax funding will play a central role for the casualties in a private insurance system, and all the problems of tax funding and what elements of care it should cover will arise again.

There is, of course, the alternative of compulsory private insurance. This is discussed by the Sutherland Commission, which asserts that there are practical objections to it. If everyone over the age of 20 had to take out personal insurance to cover their own benefits at £1000 per month after the failure of three ADLs,* the Commission computes that this would require a premium of £43.00 per month per individual. As the Commission notes, this would be a very large imposition on people on moderate incomes, particularly if put alongside the possibility of paying back student loans and the greater need to provide for personal pensions. If the compulsion were to be extended to all of those in work rather than on each individual, the expectation is that the cost would be £51.00 per month. The same considerations then apply. At the same time, there is very little public support for such an approach, with 80 per cent of people surveyed opposed to the idea. Among the crucial 25–54 year age group, only 11 per cent supported the idea.

These objections seem to be fatal enough, but it is perhaps worth noting in passing that this sort of scheme will pose exactly the same problems noted so far in the discussion. The aim of the scheme is to secure a right to income to pay for care through an insurance contract

---

* 'Activities of Daily Living', used to measure levels of dependency.

so that the right arises out of a specific contract rather than through the status of citizenship. However, this view is in fact hollow. It seems clear enough that not every individual could possibly afford to pay £43.00 per month and government would then either have to pay the premiums of those who cannot pay or find some other way of crediting them into the scheme. As the Commission says, the people with the greatest need are the least likely to be able to afford it. These costs would have to be met out of general taxation, so at least indirectly the rights of the poor to income in relation to long-term care would derive from the tax system rather than directly through insurance. Thus, the problem would arise about whether the State would support the income needed for the full package of care secured by the insurance system for those who were paying or whether it would be at a more residual level. This question would raise issues about common standards of citizenship and equality of citizenship. Also, there would obviously also be questions of means-testing – at what level of income would the State step in to pay the premiums? – and questions of discretion arising from that. In addition, as the Commission notes, to make private contributions compulsory for all of those in work at a rate of £51.00 per month would be a tax on work and would run directly counter to the Government's approach to other parts of the welfare system where benefits are being made much more conditional on work and stringently tested availability to work. So, overall, the claim that private insurance, whether voluntary or compulsory, can somehow sidestep questions about the nature of citizenship and its rights, the role of tax and what elements of care tax will fund is shown to be false.

We now turn to funding through National Insurance. Defenders of this approach argue that this is morally quite different from funding through taxation and that beliefs about entitlements account for the current sense of betrayal. The idea is that people have paid into a National Insurance scheme that has now reneged on a guarantee it was thought to embody. Again, the assumption here is that National Insurance can create a right to a specific kind of good that arises out of the quasi contract embodied in the scheme. The difficulty, however, is that this contract has never been properly spelled out in relation to the benefits that National Insurance is supposed to cover. Nor have the rates of National Insurance been computed to cover a set of clearly specified costs for long-term care or for that matter any other benefits or the health service.

The idea that National Insurance can somehow ground a right to specific kinds of benefits at specific kinds of levels seems to be illusory. Conceptually it could work only if the National Insurance system were to be kept as a pure insurance system and not, so to speak, contaminated by revenues from general taxation, since this would undermine the alleged moral principle at stake here, namely that rights can only arise out of contract. However, this would require that the National Insurance fund should be linked directly to levels of benefits payable and the level of National Insurance computed and required to be paid in relation to this supposed pure link between what people pay in and what they get out. It seems impossible to believe that this could ever happen and, if National Insurance were to pay for both nursing and personal care as well as residential costs for those who need them, the contributions would rise inexorably. It would certainly be a major move from the present system which, as the Commission says, is funded in such a diverse and complex way that it is more or less impossible to figure out how much public money – or for that matter private money – is actually going to fund long-term care.

In circumstances in which even this is not known and when both tax receipts and National Insurance resources are being used in this kind of mishmash of funding, it seems absurd to think that the funding of long-term care could become wholly funded out of National Insurance in pursuit of the will-o'-the-wisp idea that only insurance contracts or quasi contracts can actually generate rights.

Restoring trust in government

The overall message of this chapter is that there is no way of avoiding the deep questions raised by a 'tax and citizenship-based' approach to these issues. Equally, however, there is no way in which these problems about what sorts of goods should be funded, what should be left to private responsibility, and what constitutes a just or fair share in resources can be resolved by invoking moral principles independently of politics. These have to be a matter of political dialogue in an attempt to secure consent.

However, it is centrally important to restore trust in government since people do have a sense that their expectations have been betrayed, though it is essential to be honest with people about this. If we are going to be sticking to a basically tax-funded approach to long-term care then there can be no long-term guarantees. It cannot be assumed that future generations will honour obligations to which they have not consented. Equally, the level of taxation in the present generation is a matter of political controversy and the calls for lower levels of tax, particularly under the impact of globalisation and competitive pressures, have to be taken into account. Given the necessary link between tax and basic standards of citizenship, the only way of trying to secure a more predictable and lasting basis for long-term care might be through the hypothecation of about half of the receipts of income tax to fund the health service and to treat long-term care as part of this hypothecated budget. This would go some way to restoring trust that government would actually keep the funding going and for the purposes for which it was intended. Such hypothecation of the health budget was suggested recently in *Paying for progress*,[61] the report of the Fabian Tax Commission that I chaired and which reported in November 2000. This proposal, which was very controversial within the Commission, was surprisingly well received in the Press and by the Department of Health (but not the Treasury). It remains true, however, that this cannot bind future generations into the scheme. While it would be hypothecated, and thus people would have a degree of confidence that such tax would be used to fund health and health-related expenditure such as long-term care, it would still be pay-as-you-go.

Given uncertainties about the tax basis of long-term care and the need to avoid a sense of betrayal again, it seems important that tax should be used to fund the core element of the service. It would then be more likely to be clear what the State was paying for and that this payment would be sustainable for future generations. It is for these reasons that I support the Government's approach since I have become convinced by Lord Lipsey's view that the Royal Commission has made very optimistic assumptions about the long-term costs of paying for personal care. It is important that we do not make too many demands on future generations, otherwise the sense of betrayal will occur again if such future generations renege on a commitment that was based on far too rosy a picture of future costs. There is deep distrust of government, and there is deep distrust of government's ability to spend money wisely and to plan for long-term commitments. We cannot, as I have argued, avoid government taking the absolutely central role in the funding of long-term care and into the very long term. It is therefore vitally important the Government does not claim too much or allow its reach to exceed its grasp, otherwise the funding of future care may be jeopardised by the unwillingness of future generations to pay the costs.

Chapter 4

Future expectations of care in old age

Hilary Land

This chapter will address the question of how we, as a society, are
going to provide and fund care for pensioners in the future.
In exploring the answers to this question I shall be including those
who are already pensioners, many of whom are currently active and
providing care for others but who in 10 or 20 years' time may need
considerable care themselves. It is important to remember that
pensioners today are not a homogenous group, not only because they
represent a broad age span covering three or even four decades, but
also because their economic, family and health circumstances may
differ considerably. The circumstances of future generations of
pensioners will also be diverse, reflecting their different experiences of
employment, marriage, family and health, etc. Indeed, one of the key
questions for policy-makers and the wider public is just how far the
future quality, level and availability of care will depend on older
people's earlier life experiences and opportunities.

As a background to this question the chapter will:

- outline briefly the demographic and economic characteristics of
  the current generation of pensioners and identify in which key
  aspects tomorrow's pensioners are likely to be similar or different
- examine the mechanisms currently used to pay for the care of older
  people and the future impact of a changing balance between public
  and private funding
- consider the factors determining the future provision of care by
  relatives, volunteers or paid employees

- identify groups of older people and carers who are going to be most vulnerable as a result of pensions, health and social care, and employment policies
- consider experience overseas and the likely future influence on British social policy of developments in the European Union and elsewhere.

Demographic and social change

Over the past century the UK has been ageing and this trend is going to continue (see Table 4.1).

Table 4.1 Projected population, age distribution, United Kingdom, 2001–2051

	2001	2011	2021	2031	2041	2051
0–15	20%	18%	18%	17%	17%	17%
16–29	18%	18%	17%	16%	16%	16%
30–44	23%	20%	19%	19%	18%	18%
45–59	19%	21%	21%	18%	19%	18%
60–74	13%	15%	17%	19%	17%	17%
75+	7%	8%	9%	11%	13%	14%
Median age	38	41	42	43	44	44
Number (000s)	59,954	61,773	63,642	64,768	64,781	64,089

Source: Shaw, 2001; Table 1

These figures are sometimes interpreted by British politicians and journalists as being thoroughly alarming and are therefore used to justify a reduction in State commitment to pay both for pensions and for care, except in a very 'targeted' way. At first sight it looks as if an ever-growing number of old people is going to be supported by a dwindling number of people of working age. There are, however, two important points to bear in mind when looking at this table.

First, as the demographer David Coleman explains:

The UK population structure was for many years, with Sweden's, the oldest in Europe. Thanks to that, much of the pain of population ageing in the UK is already over. The proportion of the UK population aged over 64 trebled from 1901 to 1996.[62]

Other European countries are not as well placed demographically as the UK.

Second, it is a mistake to make simple comparisons between the numbers of older people and the working age population, and to estimate a 'dependency' ratio expressed in the terms of so many (or so few) working people supporting so many older people. Quite apart from the difference that patterns of migration can make to overall population size (and, in the short run, the age distribution), the size of the working population is not determined simply by the numbers in particular age cohorts. As a member of the Government Actuary's Department explained:

The attempt to define the working age population is somewhat arbitrary. In reality retirement starts at a range of different ages. Further, altering fertility or migration levels, or changing retirement age, are not the only ways of changing the number of people of working age. Indeed, research shows that changes in workforce participation rates have in the past been a more important factor than demographic trends in influencing real (economic) dependency.[63]

In other words, 'measures such as raising workforce participation rates or discouraging early retirement are likely to remain a more practical tool for increasing the working population than attempting to influence demographic behaviour'. Unemployment rates are also important.

Recently the UK government has been encouraging workers to stay in paid employment longer. The pension age for women has been increased to 65 years for all those born after 1950, and attempts are being made to reverse the trend towards 'early' retirement that (with explicit government encouragement) had developed over the past 20 years. However, as will be discussed below, increasing economic participation rates, particularly for women aged 45 years and over, do have implications for the supply and availability of informal carers.

It is clear that increasing life expectancy means there will be a higher proportion of the very old among pensioners than in the past. How much healthier they will be at the ages of the current 80 and 90 year olds is not clear: 'The evidence on the health of future elders is somewhat mixed. Thus, it is premature to assume that tomorrow's elderly will be healthier than today's.'[64]

The family experience of current pensioners is also variable. Marriage rates among women in the 1930s were higher than those in the 1920s (who now comprise the very old). Among those born in the 1940s, marriage rates have been extremely high compared with previous as well as later cohorts. Moreover, these marriages occurred at a very young age followed quickly by the birth of children. The numbers of births in the UK peaked at nearly a million in 1964 and only 5 per cent were to unmarried women. This cohort will be retiring over the next decade, with very different marriage and childbearing experiences compared with today's young women. For example, in 1973 nearly 70 per cent of women in their late 20s were married and had children. The comparable figure in 1996 was 31 per cent.[65] It is estimated that between 15 per cent and 20 per cent of women born after 1970 will remain childless. The number of marriages has fallen by 40 per cent since the 1970s to the lowest this century and, on current figures, 40 per cent of marriages will end in divorce.[66] As will be discussed below, the most important informal carers in old age are spouses and children. These figures therefore raise important questions about the commitment cohabitees will feel to care for each other in old age, as well as the commitment children will feel towards an elderly parent with whom they have lived for only part of their childhood.

On average, pensioners' incomes have increased, but one in eight pensioners is still dependent on means-tested income support (IS).[67]

The poorest are those who are entitled to IS but are not claiming it (estimated to be 500,000–870,000). The majority of the poorest pensioners are older women living alone. It is estimated that by 2025 the average pensioner's income will have increased by half as much again compared with 1997. Single pensioners will gain 66 per cent and married couples 48 per cent. While the introduction of the Minimum Income Guarantee should in theory raise the income of those at the bottom of the income distribution, in practice take-up rates among those currently eligible but not claiming are very low so far (less than one in six), despite a large and costly advertising campaign.

The proposed pensioners' tax credit will also help pensioners with modest incomes and savings. Stakeholder pensions are supposed to help those with modest incomes but these will not be fully developed until 2050. Only then will the combined basic and State pension be worth in relation to average earnings as much as the basic State pension was in 1980.[68]

All of these policies have been announced since the publication of the report of the Royal Commission on Long Term Care. Nevertheless, the conclusion drawn by the House of Commons Social Security Committee reporting in July 2000 was very similar to that of the Royal Commission. They both agreed that, despite increased prosperity for the average pensioner, 'it would be complacent to think that disparities in the incomes of older and younger pensioners and between retired men and women are set to disappear (although they may narrow). However, the oldest look set to remain among the poorest and particularly the oldest women.'[69]

The growing inequality in earnings will be reflected in inequalities in pensions. Index-linking the basic State pension to average earnings – together with SERPS – was designed to guarantee *all* pensioners a share in national prosperity. Sadly, this strategy has been abandoned. The Minimum Income Guarantee, together with the stakeholders pension and the pensioner tax credit, are likely to act as a ceiling rather than a firm foundation on which to build an adequate pension income. At the end of the 1990s, a third of employees had made contributions only to the basic State pension, but even those with occupational or personal pensions will find their income declining relative to average earnings because at best they are index-linked to prices. It cannot be assumed, therefore, that in future most pensioners will be able to afford to pay for long-term care from their own resources.

Paying for care

The Royal Commission on Long Term Care was appointed in 1997, soon after the Labour government was elected. Throughout the 1980s and 1990s, the funding of long-term care had become more and more problematic. The Royal Commission rejected private insurance as a solution. It proposed to separate living and housing costs from personal care and recommended that personal care should be free, depending on an assessment of need and *not* on a means test. Living and housing costs would remain subject to a means test. The Government has rejected the majority Commissioners' proposals on personal care and the line between health and personal care remains.

In future, old people needing personal care and domiciliary help will be expected to pay, subject to a means test. It is not yet clear at what level the means test will be set, although there may be greater consistency between local authorities. However, if overall funding is insufficient then local authorities will have to limit the services provided. There are some very important questions concerning the interaction of the various means-tested benefits and credits. If the means test is set too close to the level of the Minimum Income Guarantee, the penalty on having savings and a modest private or stakeholder pension will be greater and it may undermine the purpose of the pensioner credit, which is to reduce this penalty. This is an important question not just for the old people needing care but also because, as the Minister of State explained to the Social Security Committee:

We are trying ... to make sure what we do for today's pensioners does not wreck the long term policies for tomorrow's. We have to do it in a way that we do not say to people 'It does not pay to save' ... Whatever we do today for today's pensioners has to work to send the right signal to today's twenty and thirty year olds. If we send the wrong signal we are in real trouble.[70]

It therefore seems very likely that pressure to use a generous means test for entitlement to personal care will grow rather than diminish in the next ten years. If, however, public funding to respond to this pressure is not forthcoming then the pressure on informal carers to care for their elderly relatives will also grow. It is no accident that the Government has also begun to address the needs of carers in a more significant way than in the past. Whether or not carers will respond to these signals in the way intended remains to be seen. As discussed below, more fundamental changes may be needed.

Carers

Most of the care for older people is provided from within the family. See Tables 4.2 and 4.3 below.

As Table 4.2 shows, nearly half of all informal carers in 1995 were aged between 45 and 64. Husbands and wives are the most likely of all carers to provide help with both domestic and personal care tasks (see Table 4.3 below) and the number of hours of care they provide is considerable (see Table 4.4 below).

Table 4.3 also shows that health and personal social services provide help with personal care tasks and bathing.

Table 4.5 below shows that elderly pensioners living alone are more likely to receive considerably more support than those living with a spouse. This picture, based on figures from the mid-1990s, is very similar to the patterns found by Emily Grundy when she reviewed

Table 4.2 Characteristics of people providing informal care, GB 1995

	All carers %
Carers:	
Men	40
Women	60
Aged:	
16–44	32
45–64	48
65+	20
Dependant's relationship to carer:	
Spouse	19
Parent/parent-in-law	43
Child (any age)	9
Other relative or friend	28
Total	**100**

Source: Royal Commission on Long Term Care 1999, *Research Vol. 1.*

Table 4.3 Sources of support by type of task (percentages), England only, 1995

Sources of support	Domestic tasks %	Personal care tasks %	Bathing %
Spouse	53	66	42
Other members of the household	12	21	11
Relatives outside the household	27	3	20
Friends, neighbours	10	1	2
Voluntary workers	1	0	1
Health or personal social services	7	12	22
Paid help	1	0	0
Total (percentage of sample)	62	3	7

Source: Royal Commission on Long Term Care 1999, *Research Vol. 1.*

Table 4.4 Numbers of hours spent caring per week (for all dependants) by sex of carer, GB 1995

Hours spent caring*	Men %	Women %	Total %	Approximate numbers (millions)
0–4	31	23	26	1.5
5–9	20	23	21	1.2
10–19	19	22	21	1.2
20–49	17	17	17	1.0
50+	14	15	15	0.8

Source: Royal Commission on Long Term Care 1999, *Research Vol. 1.*

* includes time when carer was available in case help was needed. There are an estimated 5.7 million carers (3.3 million women and 2.4 million men).

research on this subject in the mid-1980s and early 1990s:[71] 'Where elderly disabled people share their households with others, household members perform virtually all of the necessary personal and domestic care tasks for them, and State services are provided at a very low level.'[72] Evidence from the Personal Social Services Research Unit to the Royal Commission concluded that only a fifth of dependant elderly people were receiving home care and only a quarter of the most dependant were doing so.[73] However, only those looking after someone for 35 hours a week and receiving the Attendance Allowance will be eligible for these services, i.e. those involved in the 'heavy end' of caring.

The Government is aware of carers' need for more help. For example, the Invalid Care Allowance has been increased and can be combined with weekly earnings of £72.00. There is now a carers' premium for those on income support, for example, and a carers' pension. Gordon Brown is proposing to extend the Invalid Care Allowance to those over 65 years. In part, this reflects the greater priority given to supporting frail old people in 'the community' who would otherwise be in residential care, for only those looking after someone for at least 35 hours a week who receives the Attendance Allowance will be eligible.

Table 4.5 Use of some health and social services by sex and household type: percentages, all aged 65+, GB 1994

	Living with spouse only		Living alone	
Type of service	Female %	Male %	Female %	Male %
District nurse/ health visitor	4	3	10	7
Home help (local authority)*	4	3	15	11
Home help (private)	5	5	10	9
Meals-on-wheels	1	1	5	7
Day centre	1	2	6	5

Source: General Household Survey 1994, ONS
* home help/home care used interchangeable by local authorities. The GHS used the term 'home help' in the question.

Table 4.6 Use of some health and social care services in the month before interview by age: percentages, GB 1994

Type of service	65–74	75+	All aged 65+
	%	%	%
District nurse/health visitor	3	11	6
Home help (local authority)*	3	15	8
Home help (private)	4	11	7
Meals-on-wheels	1	5	3
Day centre	2	3	3

Source: General Household Survey 1994, ONS
* home help/home care used interchangeable by local authorities. The GHS

Yet focusing exclusively on the needs of those who are sole or main carers means that preventative services become less of a priority and the range of support and help available is reduced. In addition, people may be deterred from asking for help at all if services are regarded as available only to people in desperate need. The aim of the strategy to create a broader more inclusive picture of caring will not be realised as long as the emphasis is on the 'heavy end'.[74]

The Government's proposals outlined in *Caring for carers* are estimated to cost £140 million – around half of the £300 million for the measures recommended by the Royal Commission. Better information and advice and respite care for carers are valuable, but they need a wider range of support and will need adequate funding. Suggestions that services should be provided on the basis of assessments that are 'carer blind' have not been taken up. Such a policy would offer help irrespective of who was available, so that the elderly person and the carer(s) would have some choice about how much and what kind of help they received. This would be particularly valuable for minority ethnic families who may prefer a different pattern of care.

Those in employment need employers who recognise the demands on their time and allow them flexibility concerning periods of paid leave as well as a right to shortened hours without being penalised with lower pay, reduced promotion chances, etc. The Government is beginning to address these issues with respect to parents with young children:[75] unpaid leave for 'family emergencies' introduced at the end of 2000 is a very timid step in the right direction. Unlike some other EU countries, establishing the *right* to work shorter hours because of family responsibilities is being successfully resisted by employers in the UK.

Some of those who gave evidence to the Royal Commission, including carers' organisations, contended 'that the limit of carers' ability to cope has been reached'.[76] Others have pointed to the fact that, despite the growing number of women joining the labour market over the past decades, informal care is not on the decline.[77] That does not mean, however, that informal carers find it easy to combine paid employment with care. It is therefore important to identify those trends that are likely to have an impact on the availability of carers as well as their capacity and commitment to care. These include trends in household and family formation, employment patterns, including the length of the working day and the location of employment in relation to home, and retirement policies as well as housing, transport and health policies.

Carers in the future

First, there are some demographic trends that will continue to have an impact on older people in a fairly direct manner. For example, the continuation of differential mortality rates between men and women means that women are much more likely to experience living alone when they are very old. The impact of other trends is not so easy to predict. For example, as discussed above, more of those reaching pension age in 25 years' time will do so without a spouse or children than those about to retire in the next ten years. In this respect they will be more similar to those women who reached pension age 25 years ago. Given that it is predicted they will also be poor, it is important that care is available to them in an acceptable way.

The growing trend towards cohabitation as a substitute for, rather than a prelude to, marriage is too recent to assess the impact this will have on informal care. Relationships based on cohabitation appear to be more fragile than those based on marriage.[78] Janet Finch has argued that:

> *The dominant way in which marriage is viewed suggests that most people would see the responsibility to provide care as an intrinsic part of this relationship and that this would be whether the marriage is the first or fourth ... The limited evidence available on spouse care would suggest this is equally true of husbands and wives.*[79]

Will cohabitation be as reliable as marriage in this respect? What about relationships that are not based on co-residence?

In the past 30 years, there have been two interesting trends concerning the households in which young people are found. First:

> *The rate of co-residence of 16 to 25 year olds with friends or other adults trebled over the last quarter century, and grew six fold for those aged 26 to 35. Just one fifth of all adults below the age of 36 now live in this form of household.*[80]

In addition, youth unemployment encouraged movement away from the family home, as our housing benefit system penalises co-residence if parents or adult children are unemployed and encourages co-residence of under-25s with non-kin. Traditional family strategies for sharing resources during times of poverty have thus been undermined by social policies in the UK as adult children are having fewer opportunities to experience reciprocity within the family. Moreover, in the past the adult child who ended up looking after elderly parents was the one who for various reasons went on living at home. On the other hand, with the expansion of higher education, students from poorer families are more likely to remain living at home than better-off students.

Second, there has been an increase of young people living alone. In 1971, only 3 per cent of 25–29-year-old men lived alone; by 1991 this had increased to 11 per cent. The comparable figures for women were 2 per cent and 6.5 per cent.[81] This is an urban phenomenon, confined almost entirely to the professional and managerial classes. It is related to wider socio-economic and occupational changes as well as the housing market and personal reasons concerning relationship breakdown. These young people are affluent, likely to have generous pensions and will be used to living alone when they retire. Altogether, 40 per cent of people living alone in 1991 were under 60 years of age, compared with 32 per cent in 1971.

The increase in economic activity rates among women has been well documented, although more attention has been paid to those with young children than those with responsibilities for caring for an older person. Today, two-thirds of women aged between 50 and 60 years are in paid employment, compared with half in the mid-1960s.[82] And now younger women will be expected to stay in the labour market until they are 65 years old. In other words, those age groups that currently provide the greatest proportion of informal care are more, rather then less, likely to have paid employment outside the home than their mothers did. The impact on their availability to care will depend on a

Table 4.7 Average length of the working week in 1982 and 1995, GB

Hours spent	Full-time		Part-time	
work & travel	Male	Female	Male	Female
1982	45.3	40.7	20.7	22.4
1995	53	48	28	26

Source: CSO, *Social Trends 1983,* p 147 and CSO, *Social Trends 1996,* p 216

number of factors, however, and there are two key trends that are in danger of undermining the capacity of carers to care.

The first relates to the relentless lengthening of the working day (see Table 4.7). In the UK, working hours and journeys to work have lengthened, so men *and* women are spending more time out of the home.

This reduces the amount of time *and* energy available for caring. Britain has the longest working hours in Europe and their reduction is not even on the political agenda. In France, a reduction of the working week to 35 hours for all and in the Netherlands to 32 hours for parents are seriously being pursued. Family-friendly policies in the UK *must* be based on a shorter working week if they are to have a positive effect on all those who have caring responsibilities.

Unlike in the 1950s, part-time and 'flexible' employment has mainly been offered to suit employers' rather than employees' needs. Perhaps the reduction in unemployment levels and the shortage of workers in health, education and social services, for example, will make employers more willing to offer employment that takes account of their employees' needs. However, in the public sector in particular this will not happen without additional resources to reverse the 'downsizing' that has occurred in the past 25 years.

The second trend is less tangible but no less important. Over the past 20 years there has been a growing emphasis placed on work – meaning paid work in the labour market – as the badge of citizenship. 'Work for those who can, security for those who cannot' is the slogan. A reduction in the unemployment rate is very welcome, for unemployment is wasteful both to society and to the individuals concerned. However this emphasis on activity in the labour market is devaluing and rendering even less visible the work of caring in the home – work that Beveridge described as 'vital although unpaid'.

This government talks a lot about community and the importance of voluntary work without seeing how corrosive of both is the emphasis they place on paid employment. There is a failure to understand that care, if it is to be safe, takes place within a relationship. Relationships take time to develop and sustain. An intrinsic part of caring is the *presence* of the carer. An example of this failure to understand the nature of informal care can be found in a recent government report on the over-50s.

In April 2000, the Government's Performance and Innovation Unit published a report on the over-50s, highlighting the ways in which 'economic trends, prevailing attitudes and demographic changes are all contributing to a structure where increasing numbers of over-50s are being written off – by employers, by society and by themselves'. Unemployment among the over-50s, it was estimated, was costing £16 billion in lost GDP each year.[83] The report showed that nearly half of the over-50s received most of their income from State benefits, and half of these were on sickness or disability benefits, and a third were not in paid work, although a quarter of workless (sic) older women were looking after family or home.

The focus of the report was the under-activity of the over-50s. As well as not being as active as they should be in the labour market, they were not doing much voluntary work: only 40 per cent of those aged 55–64 years were involved, compared with 60 per cent of all adults in the UK. However this is not surprising, given that nearly 40 per cent of this age group were concerned about the expenses of volunteering, and others believed that volunteers were providing welfare 'on the cheap' and perceived that the benefit system discouraged them from involvement in voluntary work.[84] The extent of 'informal volunteering' (i.e. volunteering that is not organised through or for an organisation) was considerable. Nearly four out of five (77 per cent) were involved in activities such as helping family, friends or neighbours with visiting, shopping, babysitting, decorating or gardening, as well as environmental work. They were a third more likely than the average adult to be visiting an elderly or sick person. This did not, however, impress the authors of the report, who are concerned to develop 'a new culture in which older people are more valued in work'. Sadly, the activities they include in the definition of 'work' are only those found in the formal employment or organised voluntary sectors. These regular, perhaps daily, visits to an old person from a familiar friend may be as important to their morale and sense of well-being as the hurried visit of the home care assistant.[85]

Overseas experiences

The question of how to provide support and care for older people if they become frail and ill is confronting all countries in the EU. Their responses have been varied and cannot be explained simply in terms of demography and economics. The conclusion drawn from the review of overseas experience collected for the Royal Commission on Long Term Care was that:

> It is striking that there appears to be little connection between the generosity of long-term care funding and beliefs about sustainability. Germany has introduced extra funding when their demographic situation is one of the more ageing in the world. Denmark has least qualms and the most expensive system. New Zealand continues to have concern about a highly rational and targeted health and long-term care system. It would appear that sustainability is a fairly elastic concept or at least nationally specific. Political views differ on what steps should be taken to sustain programmes as does public support.[86]

Where there is a strong public commitment to social care services, such as in Scandinavia, where pensioners are *not* among the poor, it has been possible to increase charges for services over time. In Denmark, adult children are *not* expected to care for their elderly parents, who have a *right* to social care. In Germany, the social care insurance scheme introduced in 1995, with a new long-term care entitlement, includes allowances to encourage family carers (mainly women) to leave employment.[87] France has developed care services and supported carers employed in the home to create jobs as well as to meet the needs of elderly people needing domiciliary services. There are concerns, however, even in Denmark, about the pay and conditions of carers as well as the standards of care on offer.

However, Britain does not look to EU countries for models of social policy development (although Scotland may develop a different approach). Increasingly, the Government has looked to Australia, New Zealand, the United States and Canada, i.e. the Anglo-Saxon nations characterised by 'liberal' welfare regimes.[88] These regimes are characterised by heavy reliance on means-tested rather than universal benefits and services. Overall it seems unlikely, therefore, that in the next 10–20 years there will be either a straightforward convergence in social policies in this area within the EU overall or, if that were to happen, that Britain would fall in line. Unless Britain's stance both towards Europe and towards State welfare provision were to change dramatically, this would not necessarily have a significant impact on policy development here.

What is clear on reviewing overseas experience is that highly targeted and means-tested systems puts carers in a double bind:

> *While caring at home, services are targeted on those without carers. If they cannot continue, the assets their spouses or parent may have wished to pass on are used up. In effect they pay twice, once by giving free care and then again by loss of inheritance. Families lucky enough to avoid the need for care gain twice. Some balancing of the risk and cost through public programmes seems only equitable.[89]*

More generally, comparative studies show that where welfare provision is limited to those too poor to rely on the market to provide their needs or whom the family has failed, provision is not popular: 'Targeted programmes enjoy much less popularity than do universal benefits ... The more comprehensive and universal, the larger is the population whose entire life course calculation is premised on social entitlements.'[90] Historical studies of the development of the Welfare States in Europe draw similar conclusions.[91] There is, therefore, a danger that the increasing emphasis on 'targeted' services based on an assessment of means rather than need more broadly defined, will result in services in which only the poor will have an interest. Without what Frank Field called 'the sharp elbows of the middle classes' to ensure decent standards are maintained, these services become second class and those who use them and work in them feel second-class citizens. This view contrasts with those who argue that by 'targeting' resources on poor pensioners, the Government is ensuring that even those without adequate incomes will be able to receive the benefits and services they need. However, quite apart from the signal this gives to the younger generation, who are being exhorted to save for their old age starting in their 20s, the message being received by pensioners themselves is very different from the one they were receiving from government when they were young. For them, means tests are complex and stigmatising, hence the poor take-up of the Minimum Income Guarantee.

The economy of welfare has always been a mix of support from the family, the market and the State. However the balance has shifted, and the current generations of pensioners and those brought up in the 1950s and 1960s not only have different *expectations* of the State but many are not *practised* in using a different welfare mix, particularly with respect to social care. There are important social class and cultural differences. As Baldock and Ungerson argue, 'the emergence of a satisfactory mixed-economy of care will require that people behave not according to the established 'grain' of everyday life, but that will mean that many of them have to make considerable adaptations'.[92] They go on:

What has been misunderstood is that effective participation by needy people in the mixed economy of care requires that they change values and assumptions that are quite fundamental to how they have lived their daily lives hitherto. We have called these 'habits of the heart', in order to emphasise how deeply embedded they are in people's existence.

Conclusion

The Royal Commission on Long Term Care, with its proposal for free personal care funded out of general taxation, provided the Government with an opportunity 'to re-establish a degree of faith in the tax system and to strengthen the public's willingness to pay for public services, assuming that the money is spent well and effectively and people can see that this is so'.[93]

It is deeply regrettable that the Government has not taken this opportunity, because the older generation's sense of betrayal in government and public services has not been dispelled. This, together with the failure to retain the earnings link to the basic State pension, has undermined their trust. Richard Titmuss pointed out 30 years ago that universalism and an infrastructure of universal services 'provides a general system of values and a sense of community'.[94] If universalism is being abandoned, what are the alternative mechanisms for ensuring a sense of community and shared responsibility between the generations? If we do not *either* restore universalism *or* find an alternative way of sustaining solidarity across the generations, the losers in the future will be not only the poorer pensioners and their carers (the majority of both being women) but all of us.

Chapter 5

What is fair in long-term care?

Justin Keen and Chris Deeming

Introduction

Equity has been a touchstone in the long-term care debate over the last few years. All sides have agreed that the current system is inequitable, implying that any proposals for reform should make it more equitable. There is a problem, though, because different inequities are emphasised by the various participants in the debate, and there is no generally agreed framework for discussing them.

This chapter argues that it is useful to disentangle equity from other issues – such as efficiency and affordability – and interpret the current long-term care debate as being about competing notions of equity. Our starting point is the Royal Commission on Long Term Care, whose report was published in the spring of 1999. It sets out the contours of the debate up to 1999, highlighting the many points of agreement and the main differences between the major protagonists in the debate. The report is studded with references to equity, and includes specific recommendations intended to make long-term care more equitable.

That said, the Commissioners did not always make their equity judgements explicit. This chapter seeks to deconstruct the arguments set out by the Royal Commission – and the Government in its response to the Commission – by abstracting them and setting them out in a conceptual framework. The framework is based on three observations. First, it is argued that there is not one debate within long-term care but a linked set of debates. Second, each debate involves discussion of different dimensions of equity – so that, for example, arguments about equal access to services are prominent in one area, while the equity of different ways of financing long-term care dominates elsewhere. Third, the long-term care debate cannot be disentangled from wider public policy debates, such as on taxation policy. The framework is used to probe the Labour government's position and to highlight the difficulties involved in making progress in the current policy context.

The Royal Commission, equality and equity

The Royal Commission on Long Term Care was clear about its commitment to finding a fairer way of financing and providing services. The concluding section of *With respect to old age* states that:

> *This report … is about a better and fairer split between costs met by the individual and the state. It is about allowing people to stay in their own homes for as long as they are able, and improving the lives of those older people who need care, and those who care for them.*[95]

Statements about the nature of the 'better and fairer split' occur throughout the main report (we turn to the dissenting note later). They are usefully grouped under four headings: payment for social services; the provision of personal care; the relationship between State and individual financing; and the role of personal income and assets in financing long-term care.

To take the first heading, there is general agreement that there are unacceptable variations in payment for a range of social services. A number of reports have highlighted the variations in charging between local authorities, and sometimes within the same authority, for home care, meals-on-wheels and other services.[96,97,98] The Commission noted the evidence about these variations, and concluded that they were unacceptable on the grounds of inconsistency. In other words, they were arguing that charging, if it were to be used at all, should be applied equally to everyone in similar circumstances. The Commission went further, however, and proposed that all personal care should be free – so that there would be no charges and hence no inconsistency in the future.

The second heading concerns the provision of personal care. The recommendation of the majority Commissioners that personal care should be free – and the disagreement of two Commissioners and the Government about it – has generated extensive comment since 1999. The Royal Commission report contrasts free treatment of cancer and heart disease within the NHS with the financial costs that can be incurred by people with Alzheimer's disease. It states that:

> ... the distinction between the way care is offered for different diseases has no justification. The situation must be put right. The proposal to exempt personal care costs from means-testing would do that ... The principle of equal care for equal needs would be properly recognised for the first time.[99]

The obvious reading of this passage is that the key principle here is equal care for equal needs – or equality of financing. However, there is an alternative interpretation, which stems from the majority Commissioners' proposals to remove means-testing and make personal care free. Free universal care for people with cancer, heart disease and Alzheimer's disease would mean that people with different needs would receive different care packages tailored to those needs. That is, there would be unequal care for unequal needs. This is a statement that equity of provision is important. Equity is concerned with the unequal distribution of resources or qualities within society – unequal distributions can be fair if the pattern of distribution ameliorates an important inequity.[100] (This type of argument is also referred to as one of vertical equity, and contrasts with horizontal equity.)

Furthermore, currently the amount you pay and the way you pay it (e.g. in cash or via general taxation) depends on the type of problem you have. According to the Commission this should not be the case. If all personal care is paid for through general taxation, as the Commission recommended, then its financing would be more progressive. Better-off people pay more taxes and will contribute more to the costs of long-term care than less well-off people. This is a statement that equity of financing is important – and in this case the measure is the extent to which a financing system is progressive. In practice, therefore, the majority Commissioners were arguing principally for equity of both financing and provision of long-term care to be increased.

The third heading, concerning the overall financing of long-term care, provides a clearer argument about equity of financing. In the last chapter of the main report the Commissioners state that:

> We argue that long-term care should continue to be funded from general taxation. Existing taxes that pay for public services are re-distributive ... The better off will contribute more for benefits which will be realised only if they are in need.[101]

While a social insurance system might in principle be used for progressive financing of care, the Commissioners argued that in practice the best solution for the UK is to use existing general taxation mechanisms. The system is already in place and works for the NHS.

The area that came under the fourth heading covers the use of personal assets and the effects of means-testing. The problem, as presented, is related to decisions about the numbers of people who should be entitled to free personal care:

> ... in our view the arrangements for the means test are too punitive. In particular, people with relatively modest means, for example with property or other capital worth less than £60,000, might lose all of their assets when they go into care and live for an average length of stay of three years. The system seems to impact on them to a far greater extent than those with higher levels of assets.[102]

The report argued for an increase in the threshold at which personal assets are disregarded, from £16,000 to either £40,000 or £60,000. This is an argument about equity of financing by individuals – unequal calls on the assets of people with similar incomes are unfair.

As with the arguments about personal care, there is an additional, unrecognised argument lurking under the surface of the report. An alternative reading of the Commission's position is that individuals should be able to keep more of the assets that they have accumulated during their lifetimes. This argument can be defended on the grounds that it is important to provide incentives for people to save for their retirement. The prospect of having savings taken away to pay for the catastrophic risk of long-term care reduces incentives to save, and may also lead to gaming of the means-testing rules.

If one adopts this position, though, it is necessary to think about a wider set of arguments. Judgements have to be made about the balance between encouraging people to save during their working lives (in order that they can afford a comfortable old age) against the principle of equity between generations. If people are able to pass on a substantial proportion of their accumulated assets to their children, then those children may have unfair advantages over those who inherit nothing. This is a good example of long-term care policies being inextricably linked to wider public policy issues. There are others in long-term care. For example, the proposal to use general taxation as the main source of financing of nursing and personal care also links long-term care to the broad Treasury concerns with taxation and spending. Long-term care is one budget heading; one priority among many.

Overall, the Commission's report provides some explicit indications of the equality and equity criteria that are relevant to long-term care, and implies some others. It also sets out a framework for the evaluation of the current and any future system, one of whose dimensions is fairness. (The others are choice/dignity/independence, security/sustainability/adaptability, and quality and best value.) Evaluation questions to be addressed include:

- does the funding system fulfil the reasonable expectations of older people?

- are older people, whose health is undermined by chronic disability, treated in the same way as those suffering from more acute illnesses?
- is the balance of funding between the individual and the taxpayer fair?

These are useful questions, insofar as they focus on relevant issues. They are not used, though, to develop an internally coherent framework for evaluation of the equity implications of the Commission's own proposals, or those that the Government or anyone else proposes.

Different definitions, different debates

Arguments about equality and equity are more complicated than the last section suggests. For example, there are irreducible differences between liberals, libertarians and others, who have different beliefs about the appropriate rules for the distribution of resources within societies.[103] This is not the place to go into these differences, save to note that a separate analysis would be possible, assessing the 'fit' between the majority Commissioners' and the Government's positions and particular political philosophies. This would help to highlight the basis of the value judgements and choices made by each site. Instead, we note here the central importance attached to equity by political philosophers of all persuasions, and employ general arguments about equality and equity in long-term care. In this section we examine the different ways in which resources can be distributed for long-term care, and the trade-offs between different equity objectives. This leads us to identify some of the key points of difference between the majority Commissioners on the one hand and the minority Commissioners and the Government on the other.

In long-term care three kinds of decisions need to be made. First, we have to decide what is to be distributed, and to what end. Clearly, we should be concerned with the fair distribution of something important

– but what? For the majority Commissioners the important something appears to be services, particularly formal health and social care services, though this is never completely spelled out. This is a reasonable choice in the context of long-term care, given the centrality of the issue of providing nursing and personal care. It is not, though, the only option. One alternative would be Amartya Sen's concept of equalising people's capabilities, so that they can freely choose between alternative lives.[104]

The minority Commissioners' and the Government's position is less clear. They are not specific about their equity objectives, although their implicit position is that individuals' contributions to the financing of long-term care should be according to ability to pay. That is, their main concern is with the distribution of the State's financial resources. This goes to the heart of the arguments just mentioned, because distributing different resources or capabilities requires different policy mechanisms and may lead to different allocations by the State. It would appear that there are major philosophical differences between the two sides in the long-term care debate, and these underpin the differences that are evident over means-testing and other issues.

Second, judgement criteria are required for the distribution of resources. We can usually only strive towards equity objectives, and have to judge how close we come towards them before we are content. For example, one of the founding principles of the NHS is that it should be free at the point of delivery. In fact, about 2 per cent of NHS income is raised through user charges for dentistry, prescriptions and other goods and services. This violates the principle, though not to the extent that this or any recent government in Westminster has felt impelled to remove them. (We note that, in contrast, people under 25 in Wales are now exempted from prescription charges.)

In practice, it is also necessary to make trade-offs between policy objectives. The Commission recognised the fundamental problem of balancing State and personal provision, favouring a shift towards State financing and provision of nursing and personal care, while housing and living costs were still means-tested. In contrast, the minority Commissioners and the Government prefer to make nursing care free in all settings, and continue to charge for personal care. These lead to different trade-offs. The majority Commissioners are seeking to maximise equity of provision and of individual payment (via general taxation), partly by increasing total State financing. The Government prefers to work towards more equitable State financing, both in its general welfare policies and in long-term care (though the extent to which its policies on long-term care will actually deliver is unclear). This would be at the expense of greater inequity in personal financing, since substantial costs have to be met by people on very different incomes.

Third, who does the distributing? The Commission assumed that the State was the main distributor of resources. This is a common assumption in public policy circles, and not unreasonable in the context in which the Commission was working. It is worth noting in passing, however, that there are proper questions to be asked about equity within families. The Commission and the Government appear to have relied on the observation that relatives who do the informal caring do it willingly, at least to the limits of their own ability to do that caring. This skirts round the question of which relative does the caring when more than one could do it.

In addition, families often contribute to a relative's long-term care costs. This raises questions about the fairness of families finding themselves in a position where they feel obliged to contribute, which are not properly tackled by either side. This is related to the issue, mentioned earlier, concerning equity between generations. Both the Royal Commission and the Government acknowledge the unpredictable nature of long-term care costs, but neither proposed measures to protect people's assets – or conversely to remove the assets of those lucky enough to avoid the costs of long-term care.

A conceptual framework

The debate following the Commission report suggests that this is not a straightforward area of policy to characterise. We therefore propose a conceptual framework to help clarify the terms of the debate, which is based on three observations. First, long-term care is not one debate, but several (see Figure 5.1 below). For example, there is a debate about the definitions of nursing and personal care, and whether personal care can or should be free at the point of use. There is another debate about the extent to which individuals should be required to use their private assets (including housing assets) to pay for long-term care.

Figure 5.1 Long-term care – a set of linked debates

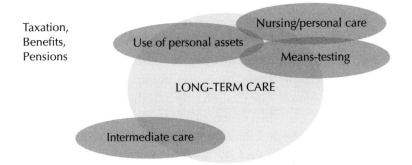

Second, the relevant equity objectives can be different in each area of the debate. Thus, the debate about free personal care revolves around the desirability of maximising equity of both financing and provision, particularly through an extension of universality. The debate about the use of personal assets, in contrast, concerns the appropriate financing principle that should be applied.

One important result is that it is possible for a given policy to increase equity in one area without affecting equity in others. Providing free personal care might have little effect on the likelihood that some people in nursing homes will exhaust their personal assets – because they will still run them down by paying for their housing and living costs. Equally, decisions about equity objectives in one area can affect policy options in other areas. Again, the obvious example is the provision of free personal care, since free provision would mean that existing variations in the financing of home care would be reduced.

The third observation is that the individual debates are linked to other major areas of social policy. If long-term care provision is financed mainly through general taxation, then it is also part of government-wide policy-making processes concerned with the uses of tax monies. If means-testing is to be retained, as the Government prefers, then all income and assets – including pensions and benefits – must be included in any discussion of the financing of long-term care. Changes in pensions and benefits policies will have implications for long-term care financing.

This leads us to a framework where there are linked debates, where particular dimensions of equity are relevant within each one, and where the individual debates are set in a wider context, which includes taxation and other wider government policies. The framework allows us to make some observations about the current state of the long-term care debate, namely:

- Some aspects of equity are clearly visible in the debate but others have been submerged.

- The result is that some aspects of the debate have not been properly examined in recent years. For example, the Commission appears to have assumed that free nursing and personal care will lead people in nursing homes to have higher net personal incomes. Will personal incomes really go up, or will nursing homes increase charges for other services, leaving individuals no better off? This assumption has not been investigated in any detail, and it is not clear whether or not it is right.

- People typically focus on one aspect of the long-term care debate without thinking through any consequences for the rest. The debate has, to say the least, been fragmented.

- The majority Commissioners and the Government are to some extent talking at cross-purposes. The majority Commissioners' proposals cover each area represented in Figure 5.1, but the minority Commissioners and the Government are most concerned with the financial implications for the State – and this concern has strongly influenced government decisions about other aspects of the long-term care debate.

Does the Government want greater equity in long-term care?

This raises the question of what the Government really wants. As we noted earlier, the Government appears to be committed to greater equity in long-term care. The main point of difference with the majority Royal Commissioners concerns the choice of the main equity objective. The majority Commissioners are driven by a desire to make provision more equitable (regardless of ability to pay) and the Government prefers to focus on public expenditure and its redistribution. In its response to the Commission, the Government stressed that 'any contribution people are asked to make to the cost of their care is fair, predictable and related to their ability to pay' and a 'fairer and lasting balance between taxpayers and individuals must be found for the funding of long term care ... to ensure that people's health care is provided squarely in line with NHS principles and they are not forced to sell their homes as soon as they enter residential care'.[105]

However, neither the rest of the response nor subsequent publications set out how the Government thinks a fairer system can be achieved. Indeed, the Government worried that:

> *Making personal care free for everyone carries a very substantial cost, both now and in the future. It would consume most of the additional resources we plan to make available for older people through the NHS Plan. Yet it would not necessarily improve services as the Note of Dissent to the Royal Commission's report makes clear.*

It does not help the least well off. We have not followed this recommendation because we believe our alternative proposals to improve standards of care and fair access to services will generate more important benefits of health and independence for all older people, now and in the future.[106]

Three points can be made about this position. First, it seems to place stress on fair access, but in practice the Government is concerned with equality of *charging*:

Not only do charging policies vary hugely, but in some councils it is the poorest members of society who are most in need of care who pay the highest charges. The Government has therefore taken a new power in the Care Standards Act to allow binding statutory guidance to be issued ...[107]

Subsequent guidance[108] shows that the Government is seeking to reduce variations in charging, in a way that will leave charging in place but make payments slightly more equitable for lower income groups. The Government cannot claim that it is concerned with fair access to services – this is precisely what it has set itself against by rejecting free personal care.

Second, the Government offers no explicit equity – that is, no distributional – principle. A concrete example helps to make this point. In spite of stating that the majority Commissioners' recommendations will not help the least well-off, the Government's own proposals do not help the least well-off either. People on low incomes who live in nursing homes already have free nursing care, but still contribute much of their income towards housing, living and personal care (see Figure 5.2). The poorest people have just £15.98 per week as 'pocket money'.

Figure 5.2 Relationship between contributions and income/assets in nursing homes

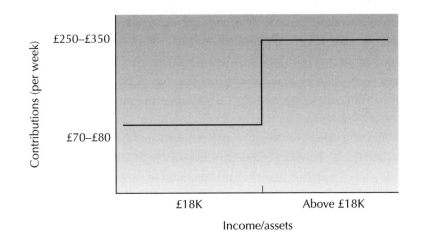

More generally, the Government has not said what it thinks would be a fair split between State and individual financing – even though it has said that this is needed – and as a result we do not know what level of payment by individuals for long-term care it considers fair. This is what we meant earlier when we said that the Government's position has not been thought through.

Third, the Government is seeking to limit the area within which it will debate. It claims that intermediate care will improve access and quality of services for older people. The problem with this position is that the Government is confounding services that are provided to different groups of people. If the Government's plans for intermediate care are realised (a big 'if' at present), then unnecessary hospital and nursing home admissions might be avoided. People in receipt of long-term care are, in practice, a different group – they may go into hospital at some point, but are really receiving a different bundle of services. So, action on intermediate care will not help most people in long-term care. The Government is therefore offering a stark political choice rather than one based on any clear criterion for deciding how to support a single, defined group of people.

The Government's position is a fudge. It is really pursuing a strategy of minimum change in long-term care. It has adopted a number of discrete policy positions within the overall debate, but there is no early prospect of major reform. Long-term care thus remains a textbook case of disjointed and incremental change being preferred to fundamental reform. One reason why the Government is able to pursue this strategy is because there has not been a clear consensus within the population at large. This situation may be changing, as evidenced by a recent opinion poll[109] revealing support for State financing of personal as well as nursing care. It remains to be seen whether this is translated into political pressure at some point in the future.

If it is, then the Government will have to make its position more explicit. If it had a coherent set of policies and was simply concealing them behind a wall of fudge, then this would not be a difficult technical task. The only problem would be the political one of changing an entrenched policy position. Our sense, though, is that the Government has developed policy positions on specific issues, but has not thought through a coherent set of policies that covers all aspects of long-term care. The Government *is* concerned about specific problems, such as unacceptable variations in charging and the risk of reducing the incomes of poorer people in nursing homes still further. But its responses to these problems are tactical rather than strategic.

Long-term care: a wicked problem

Some problems in public policy are inherently difficult to think about and manage: they are 'wicked' problems. Since the long-term care debate keeps running into the conceptual sand, it seems to be composed entirely of wicked problems. Figure 5.1 above suggested why this is the case. Any serious effort to solve a problem in one area of long-term care is likely to have important policy implications in others. This is precisely why the majority Commissioners wanted to make personal care free – they believed that it solved problems caused by the nursing/personal care divide, means-testing and perhaps variations in provision as well. It would resolve a number of policy dilemmas at once. The alternative is more incrementalism – making relatively modest changes in one area on the basis that anything more will lead to policy outcomes in others that the Government does not want. In particular, moving any further towards free care means higher costs to the State – at least in the Government's view.

Nevertheless, the arguments presented here suggest that, whatever happens next, the need is to face up to two issues. The first is practical. At present, people in work – tomorrow's pensioners – cannot reasonably be expected to understand how much money they should be putting aside to pay for long-term care. The Government has not made clear what, exactly, people might have to pay for. It is unfair to expect everyone of working age to work out what to do if the Government will not help them to do so. The Government must therefore be explicit about the chances of us needing long-term care, the amounts of money people on a particular income may have to pay if they need it, and explain the most appropriate ways of saving for any possible future costs.

The second issue is about equity. As some of the quotes reproduced here show, the Government finds it easy to use the word 'fairness' in the context of long-term care – as it does in social policy generally. As we have also seen, though, it remains unclear what form its commitment to fairness actually takes. We are driven to conclude, then, that the Government needs to demonstrate its commitment to equality and equity in concrete ways. Otherwise, its commitment will be more apparent than real.

References

1   Joseph Rowntree Foundation. *Meeting the costs of continuing care*. York: Joseph Rowntree Foundation, 1996.

2   House of Commons Health Select Committee. *Long-term care: future provision and funding: third report*. London: Stationery Office, 1996.

3   Royal Commission on Long Term Care. *With respect to old age*. London: Stationery Office, 1999.

4   Easterbrook L. *Long-term care finances: the challenges for government*. London: King's Fund, unpublished, 1999.

5   Secretary of State for Health. *The Government's response to the Royal Commission on Long Term Care*. Cm 4818-II. London: Stationery Office, 2000.

6   Secretary of State for Health. *The NHS Plan: a plan for investment; a plan for reform*. London: Stationery Office, 2000.

7   Liberal Democrat Party. *An age of opportunity: policies for older people*. London: Liberal Democrats, 2000.

8   Conservative Party. *Immediate benefit to all in Conservatives long term care plan*. Press release, 2001.

9   Deeming C. *A fair deal for older people? Public views on the funding of long-term care*. London: King's Fund, 2001.

10 Secretary of State for Health. *The New NHS: modern, dependable*. London: Stationery Office, 1997.

11 Secretary of State for Health. *The NHS Plan: a plan for investment; a plan for reform. Op. cit.*

12 Royal Commission on Long Term Care. *With respect to old age. Op. cit.*

13 Secretary of State for Health. *The Government's response to the Royal Commission on Long Term Care. Op. cit.*

14 Means R, Smith R. *From Poor Law to community care: the development of welfare services for elderly people, 1939–1971*. Bristol: Policy Press, 1998.

15 Means R, Smith R. *From Poor Law to market care: the development of welfare services for elderly people, 1971–1993*. Bristol: Policy Press (forthcoming).

16 Gilbert B. *British social policy, 1919–39*. London: Batsford, 1970.

17 Roberts N. *Our future selves*. London: Allen & Unwin, 1970.

18 Matthews O. *Housing the infirm* (self-published and distributed through W H Smith & Son, no date).

19 Amalree, Lord. *Adding life to years*. London: NCSS, 1951.

20 McEwan P, Laverty S. *The chronic sick and elderly in hospital.* Bradford Hospital Management Committee, 1949.

21 See also Means R, Smith R. *From Poor Law to community care: the development of welfare services for elderly people, 1939–71. Op. cit.*

22 Samson E. *Old age in the new world.* London: Pilot Press, 1944.

23 McEwan P, Laverty S. *The chronic sick and elderly in hospital. Op. cit.*

24 Means R, Smith R. *From Poor Law to community care: the development of welfare services for elderly people, 1939–1971. Op. cit.*

25 Quoted in Samson. *Old age in the new world. Op. cit.*

26 Quoted in Means R, Smith R. *From Poor Law to community care: the development of welfare services for elderly people, 1939–1971. Op. cit.*

27 Rowntree Report. *Old people: report of a survey committee on the problems of ageing and the care of old people.* New York: Arno Press, 1980.

28 Nuffield Provincial Hospitals Trust. *The hospital surveys: the Domesday Book of the hospital services.* Oxford: Oxford University Press, 1946.

29 Anderson Report. *The care and treatment of the elderly and infirm.* London: BMA, 1947; Amaltree. *Adding life to years. Op. cit.*

30 Rucker Report. *The break up of the Poor Law.* Public Records Office (Cabinet Papers 134/698). 1946.

31 *Ibid.*

32 Quoted in Means R, Smith R. *From Poor Law to community care: the development of welfare services for elderly people, 1939–1971. Op. cit.*

33 *Ibid.*

34 Garland R. End of the Poor Laws – and a new era dawns in British social welfare. *Social Welfare* 1948; 11 (2): 36.

35 Means R, Smith R. *From Poor Law to community care: the development of welfare services for elderly people, 1939–1971. Op. cit.*

36 Townsend P. *The last refuge.* London: Routledge & Kegan Paul, 1964.

37 Ministry of Health. *Report of the Ministry of Health for the year ended 31st December 1958.* London: HMSO, 1959.

38 Kemp M. An update on the built workhouse. *Built Environment* 1973; 2 (9): 496.

39 Townsend. *The last refuge. Op. cit.*

40 Godlove C, Mann A. Thirty years of the Welfare State: current issues in British social policy for the aged. *Aged Care and Services Review* 1980; 2 (1): 3.

41 Parker J. *Local health and welfare services.* London: Allen & Unwin, 1965.

42 Huws Jones R. Old people's welfare – successes and failures. *Social Services Quarterly* 1952; 26 (1): 19–22.

43 Means R, Smith R. *From Poor Law to community care: the development of welfare services for elderly people, 1939–1971*. Op. cit.

44 Boucher Report. *Survey of services available to the chronic sick and elderly, 1954–55*. London: HMSO, 1957.

45 Ministry of Health. *Local authority services for the chronic sick and infirm*. Circular 14/57. 7 October 1957.

46 Ministry of Health. *Geriatric services and the care of the chronic sick*. HM (57) 86, 7 October 1957.

47 Davies M. Swapping the old around. *Community Care* 1979; 18 October: 16–17.

48 Ministry of Health. *The care of the elderly in hospitals and residential homes*. Circular 18/65. 20 September 1965.

49 Secretary of State for Health. *The Government's response to the Royal Commission on Long Term Care*. Op. cit.

50 Laing & Buisson. *Laing's review of private health care, 1992*. London: Laing & Buisson, 1992.

51 Means R, Smith R. *Community care: policy and practice*. Basingstoke: Macmillan, 1998.

52 Lewis J, Glennester H. *Implementing the new community care*. Buckingham: Open University Press, 1996.

53 Avebury K. *Home life: a code of practice for residential care*. London: Centre for Policy on Ageing, 1984.

54 Means R, Smith R. *From Poor Law to market care: the development of welfare services for elderly people, 1971–1993*. Op. cit.

55 Means R, Smith R. *Community care, policy and practice*. Op. cit.

56 Saunders P. *A nation of home owners*. London: Unwin Hyman, 1944.

57 Heywood F, Oldman C, Means R. *Housing and home in later life*. Buckingham: Open University Press, 2001 (forthcoming).

58 For a rigorous argument on this point, see Nozick R. *Anarchy, state, and utopia*. Oxford: Blackwell, 1974.

59 Pinker R. *Social theory and social policy*. London: Heinemann, 1971.

60 See Nozick. *Anarchy, state, and utopia*. Op. cit.

61 Fabian Society. *Paying for progress*. London: Fabian Society, 2000.

62 Coleman D, Chandola T. Britain's place in Europe's population. In: McRae S, editor. *Changing Britain: families and households in the 1990s*. Oxford: Oxford University Press, 1999.

63 Shaw C. United Kingdom population trends in the 21st century. *Population Trends* 2001; 103: 37–46.

64 Dunnell K. Policy responses to population ageing and population decline in the United Kingdom. *Population Trends* 2001; 103: 47–52.

65 Berthoud R C. *Family formation in multi-cultural Britain: three patterns of diversity*. INSER, University of Essex, 2001.

66 Murphy M, Wang B. Forecasting British families into the twenty-first century. In McRae S, editor. *Changing Britain: families and households in the 1990s. Op. cit.*

67 Social Security Committee. *Seventh report, pensioner poverty*. HC606, July 2000. London: Stationery Office, 2000.

68 *Ibid.*

69 *Ibid.*

70 *Ibid.*

71 Grundy E. Demographic influence on the future of family care. In: Allen I, Perkins E, editors. *The future of family care for older people*. London: HMSO, 1995.

72 Arber S, Ginn J. *Gender and later life*. London: Sage, 1991.

73 Royal Commission on Long Term Care. *With respect to old age. Op. cit.*

74 Lloyd L. Caring about carers: only half the picture. *Critical Social Policy* 2000; 20 (1).

75 Department of Trade and Industry. *Work and parents: competitiveness and choice*. Cm 5005. London: Stationery Office, 2000.

76 Royal Commission on Long Term Care. *With respect to old age. Op. cit.*

77 Joshi H. The labour market and unpaid caring: conflict and compromise. In: Allen I, Perkins E. *The future of family care for older people. Op. cit.*

78 Kiernan K, Mueller G. Who divorces? In: McRae S, editor. *Changing Britain: families and households in the 1990s. Op. cit.*

79 Finch J. Responsibilities, obligations and commitments. In: Allen I, Perkins E. *The future of family care for older people. Op. cit.*

80 Gershuny J. *Household and family structure: issues for the future*. London: ESRC, 2000.

81 Hall R, Ogden P, Hill C. Living alone: evidence from England and Wales and France in the last decade. In: McRae S, editor. *Changing Britain: families and households in the 1990s. Op. cit.*

82 Hunt A. *A survey of women's employment. Report*. London: HMSO, 1968.

83 10 Downing Street Press Release, 27 April 2000.

84 *Ibid.*, 41.

85 Ostner I. The politics of care policies in Germany. In: Lewis J, editor. *Gender, social care and welfare state restructuring in Europe*. Aldershot: Ashgate, 1998.

86 Royal Commission on Long Term Care. *Research Vol. 1*. Cm 4192-II/1. London: Stationery Office, 1999.

87 Clarke H, Dyer S, Horwood J. *That bit of help: the high value of low level preventative services for older people*. Bristol: Policy Press, 1998.

88 Esping Anderson G. *Social foundation of post industrial economics*. Oxford: Oxford University Press, 2000.

89 *Ibid*.

90 *Ibid*.

91 Baldock J, Ungerson C. Money, care and consumption: families in the new mixed economy of social care. In: Jones H, Miller J. *The politics of the family*. Aldershot: Avebury, 1996.

92 *Ibid*.

93 Royal Commission on Long Term Care. *With respect to old age. Op. cit*.

94 Titmuss R M. *Commitment to welfare*. London: Allen & Unwin, 1968.

95 Royal Commission on Long Term Care. *With respect to old age. Op. cit*.

96 Baldwin S, Lunt N. *Charging ahead. The development of local authority charging policies for community care*. Bristol: Policy Press, 1996.

97 Audit Commission. *Charging with care. How local councils charge for home care*. London: Audit Commission, 2000.

98 Department of Health. *Modernising social services*. London: Stationery Office, 1998.

99 Royal Commission on Long Term Care. *With respect to old age. Op. cit*.

100 Mooney G. And now for vertical equity? Some concerns arising from Aboriginal health in Australia. *Health Economics* 1996; 5: 99–103.

101 Royal Commission on Long Term Care. *With respect to old age. Op. cit*.

102 Royal Commission on Long Term Care. *With respect to old age. Op. cit*.

103 Kymlicka W. *Contemporary political philosophy*. New York: Oxford University Press, 1990.

104 Sen A. *Inequality revisited*. Cambridge: Harvard University Press, 1992.

105 Secretary of State for Health. *The Government's response to the Royal Commission on Long Term Care. Op. cit*.

106 Secretary of State for Health. *The Government's response to the Royal Commission on Long Term Care. Op. cit*.

107 Secretary of State for Health. *The Government's response to the Royal Commission on Long Term Care. Op. cit*.

108 Department of Health. *Fairer charging policies for home care and other non-residential social services*. London: Department of Health, 2001.

109 Deeming C. *A fair deal for older people? Public views on the funding of long-term care. Op. cit*.